A BUSINESS PARABLE

HARPER'S
RULES

A RECRUITER'S GUIDE *to* FINDING *a* DREAM JOB *and the* RIGHT RELATIONSHIP

DANNY CAHILL

GREENLEAF
BOOK GROUP PRESS

Published by Greenleaf Book Group Press
Austin, Texas
www.gbgpress.com

Distributed by Greenleaf Book Group LLC

For ordering information or special discounts for bulk purchases, please contact Greenleaf Book Group LLC at PO Box 91869, Austin, TX 78709, 512.891.6100.

Design and composition by Greenleaf Book Group LLC and Bumpy Design
Cover design by Greenleaf Book Group LLC

Publisher's Cataloging-In-Publication Data
(Prepared by The Donohue Group, Inc.)
Cahill, Danny.   Harper's rules : a recruiter's guide to finding a dream job and the right relationship / Danny Cahill. -- 1st ed.   p. ; cm.
  "A business parable."
  ISBN: 978-1-60832-100-1
  1. Job hunting. 2. Employment interviewing. 3. Career development. 4. Interpersonal relations. 5. Quality of work life. 6. Parables I. Title.
HF5382.7 .H37 2011
650.14   2010940053

Part of the Tree Neutral® program, which offsets the number of trees consumed in the production and printing of this book by taking proactive steps, such as planting trees in direct proportion to the number of trees used: www.treeneutral.com

TreeNeutral®

Printed in the United States of America on acid-free paper

11 12 13 14 15 16   10 9 8 7 6 5 4 3 2 1

First Edition

CONTENTS

PROLOGUE

Since my divorce two years ago, I have become good at resisting men, and I have always been good at resisting headhunters, so when you put the two together, a male head-hunter has no chance with me. I know why they call—I am a successful software sales rep with a massive network of clients, and I'm an attractive woman. They want to know if I am happy. Would I like to hear about a dream job? But I don't think much about happiness anymore. So I don't return their calls.

Except Harper Scott.

Harper placed me eight years ago when I was first learning how to sell software, and then again a few years later. He's been a successful headhunter for a long time. He seems to know everyone in my market space and everything that is going on. Harper is connected. But that's not why I return his calls.

"Casey, it's Harper. Do you really think you can get away with this shabby treat-ment? You don't send funny emails; you don't call. I am seriously considering starting a relationship with you just so I can break up with you and have you know my pain."

I giggled. I'm thirty-four. I thought I left giggling behind.

"We need to talk. Call me. Notice I am not leaving my number. If you don't still have it, all is lost."

I told myself to ignore his message. I've been at my job for just over a year, and call-ing Harper back would mean getting caught up with the drama of interviews and the inevitable subterfuge with my current boss. Why bother?

So I held out. For about four minutes. I got his voice mail, left a message, and a few minutes later his assistant called and said Harper wanted me to meet him at one o'clock at Max's Oyster House the following Tuesday.

As I got dressed on Tuesday morning, I convinced myself that I was trying to make a good impression on the CIO that I was doing a demo for that afternoon. But why was

I reaching for the black, form-fitting cashmere sweater and the charcoal grey skirt that even I, as my backside's biggest critic, know hangs and clings in a flattering way? Why am I giving this account the full "I'm very corporate, very astute, and wicked hot" look? I pretended to recall my meeting with Harper as I put my hair up to expose my neck.

I sat in the restaurant for ten minutes before Harper showed. Nothing is more fiendishly calculated than his penchant for making everything seem uncalculated. He must be forty now, but could easily pass for younger. Flecks of grey accent his brown hair, and at six feet, he is still at fighting weight—shoulders broad, waist impossibly narrow. My friend Hannah once asked me what he looked like, and I said, "Big in the right places, small in the right places." She understood immediately.

Harper took his seat, folded his hands, placed them under his chin, and smiled at me. I looked him straight in the eyes, the same way I start any meeting, but I didn't know for the life of me why I was there.

"You're wondering why you're here. You're a busy person, you're not looking for a job, you're feeling vaguely guilty about meeting with a headhunter on company time. And yet, it's so good to see me. Am I right?"

"About everything except the 'it's so good to see you' part."

"I'm shattered."

"Bounce back, Harper. I agreed to see you because I'm in town rolling out a demo and because I was curious to see if you had gone to seed yet like most guys your age."

"And have I?"

"Not quite."

An impossibly cute, young waitress excused herself for interrupting, took our drink orders, and told us the specials. Harper asked her how she was doing, and then told her he was a headhunter and when she was ready to start a career she should look him up. I rolled my eyes as she walked away beaming.

"You're pathetic."

"Six degrees of separation," he shrugged. "My network is my lifeblood. You don't know who she knows."

"I'm ready for your pitch now, Harper. I Googled you this morning."

"Isn't that eerie? I Googled me this morning, too. Any new entries since 7 A.M.?"

Harper's ego could be a bit much, but then he redeemed himself. He took out his wallet and showed me the latest pictures of his daughter. I raved, because she really was fabulous.

"A teenager already. Has it been that long since you first recruited me?"

"Don't remind me."

He leaned back, and I could tell the icebreaking was over. He was here to qualify a prospect that could make him money. I would be well served to keep that in mind.

"So, here's what my research associate tells me. Nineteen months ago you're one of SAP's resident stars. Big territory, established key accounts, and overrides from three direct reports. W2 of over 330K. You leave and end up at an underfunded supply chain company where you'll be lucky to make 225. It doesn't add up, Casey."

"I'm not going on any interviews, Harper. I like my job."

"Were you sleeping with the boss?"

"What?! John was sixty-three, with yellow teeth and a unibrow."

"So then, what? It doesn't add up and you know it."

I promised myself I wouldn't share this. A solemn promise, made at my bathroom mirror just five hours ago, now wafting gently out the restaurant's open windows . . .

"I got divorced, okay? Don't look at me like that. It's not *that* shocking."

"No. What is shocking is that my research assistant missed it. I'd fire her, except that I'd be lost without her."

"It's no big deal. We had no kids; we both had careers. We evaluated, we made a choice, we negotiated and distributed our assets, and we moved on."

"Well, look at you and your stiff upper lip! Did you shake hands and say, 'Good luck?'"

"We did in fact shake hands. Then he said, 'Godspeed.'"

Harper leaned back. "He actually said the word 'Godspeed'? I've never been able to work that into a sentence. So you're fine? No residual sadness?"

"Nope."

Our waitress bought me some time by asking if we had any questions. Neither of us had really looked at the menu, so we both agreed to the halibut when she raved that it was "phenomenal." Harper clapped his menu shut. I reached over for my jacket, slipped my Blackberry out, and turned the power off.

"You turn thirty-five soon, right?" Harper said. "So if you're going to have a family, you need to pick one of the many guys I'm sure you're dating, shorten the engagement, and abandon all birth control."

"I'm not focused on that right now, Harper."

"There are guys, right? You're beautiful, you're smart, and you don't need their money."

His charms had run their course; I was now officially angry. I started gathering up my things.

"Have your research assistant delete me from your database when you get back to the office, Harper."

"Two minutes."

I looked at him with the half querying, half irritated expression I would use on Donald when he left wet clothes in the dryer.

"Give me two minutes," he said, "and this meeting will have been worthwhile for you, whether you eat or not."

As if on cue, the food came. I couldn't very well exit while Miss Teen America was warning me the plate was "super duper hot." I sat down.

He cut his food slowly and didn't look up while he spoke.

"Thank you, Casey. Answer me this, and remember, I only have two minutes, so don't overthink it. You traveled 85 percent of the time. He was home, a desk jockey. May I assume he cheated on you?"

Oh, what the hell . . .

"Yes. Apparently for a long time." I will not cry; I will not turn this arrogant head-hunter into Barbara Walters.

"And if one of your friends knew? If I knew? Would you have wanted to know?"

"Yes."

"You're sure? It's touchy. You reconcile and then the friend or friends who told you are the bad guys on the wrong team."

"So they said. They were wrong. They should have trusted that I would have never blamed them."

He nodded. "If you ever find out my wife is cheating, let me know."

"Right after I assure her nobody would blame her."

He smiled wanly and then emitted a slow, dense sigh.

"You're getting fired, Casey." He said it without looking at me. "Tynan is bringing in a new EVP, and he's going to clean house. Replacing the whole sales force, starting in six weeks. I'm sorry."

"How do you know?"

"I placed the new EVP. Tynan gave me the search four months ago."

"And you tell me now?"

"Ethically, I shouldn't be telling you at all. Look, Casey, your boss was going to get fired; someone was going to get that search. Any new EVP is going to bring in his own people. Because it's me, you are the only one in the sales force who knows. You have at least three or four months to prepare, plan, and find a job, and it will be better. Because I care."

I was twirling linguini drenched in pesto sauce with my fork. My stomach felt like it had jumped off a bridge. What was the point of trying to take another bite? I lowered my fork.

"Look, Casey, this is a good thing. You'll get out before they let you go; you've got a track record, leverage. In the long run, this is the best thing that could happen to you."

"Oh save it, Harper, really. Every time something bad happens to me, I am surrounded by people telling me it's the best thing that could have happened to me—none of whom, by the way, are personally affected. Donald falls in love with a co-worker's wife, a woman I introduced him to, and it's a good thing because he didn't love me, and now I can find someone who does. The fact that their affair humiliated me at work and made a cushy job untenable—a job that I had killed myself for over a decade to attain— was a good thing because at a new company there'd be no ghosts, no gossip.

"And now that I have picked myself off the floor and established myself, albeit at a crappy company, that, too, is being taken away, and you say it's the best thing for me. You know what? It's not. It's not good that I'm going to be out of a job; it's not good that I'm not dating, that I only go out to eat for business; it's not good that I am in sweats all weekend and am addicted to *Court TV* and high-glycemic foods. It is the exact opposite of good, Harper; can you let me have that for just a while? Is that too much to ask?"

"How is everything, you two?" said Miss Teen America.

"It's good," I said.

"No," Harper nearly bellowed, "it's not. It is the opposite of good, and we would just like to *experience* the food's opposite-of-goodness for a while. Is that too much to ask?" Miss Teen America withdrew, slightly dazed.

"You're an idiot, Harper."

"Yes, but an empathetic, listening idiot." He gave me the kind of smile that made me want to feel better for *him*, so that he'd keep smiling. My whole life has been spent doing whatever I need to do to keep men smiling.

"So now what?"

"You need to read my book," he said.

"You wrote a book?"

"Does that seem inconceivable?"

"On getting a job?"

"Writing a simple book on getting a job is not going to get me on Oprah's couch. It has a far more ambitious scope."

"What's it called?"

"It's called . . . I, uh, have decided to call it . . . *Harper's Rules: The Recruiter's Guide to Finding a Dream Job and the Right Relationship.*"

"You've written no such book, have you, Harper?"

"I certainly have, and I find that comment insulting. Now, to clarify, I haven't writ- ten it in the sense of having actually committed words to paper in some structured, organized form."

"In what sense then, given that tiny distinction, would it qualify as a book?"

"Continued ridicule will take you right off the dedication page. You wanted to hear a pitch, here it comes: I've been a headhunter for twenty years. I interview, I evaluate, I dig deep because I need to know how people make decisions. If they don't accept the job, I don't get paid. And here's what I've learned:

"There is no difference between making decisions in your career path and making decisions in your romantic life.

"It's the most natural analogy in the world, and one every headhunter uses. We all know an interview is like a date; we seek attractive jobs using the same skills we use to find a mate; the best relationships come through referrals; giving notice feels like breaking up; and as you now know, getting fired feels like you've been cheated on. Get the premise, or do I go on?"

I found myself remembering previous interviews: how I sized up the staff members I met—how dull or funny they seemed, the office zeitgeist. It was like walking into a party.

"My book is meant for someone just like you," he said. "You are my target audience. Usually we're happy in our relationships but our career is in trouble, or we love our job but our home life is terrible, so we gravitate toward the positive reinforcement of one or the other. The problem gets exacerbated because a loved one or a boss feels ignored."

I put my napkin on the table and folded my hands in front of me. I would have liked nothing better than to shoot Harper down, but my thoughts flashed to evenings on the road, sitting at a Marriot bar with the other road warriors, and how quickly the conversation descended into the ingratitude of a spouse left at home or the unfair expectations of a CIO changing the specs on an order. Given enough alcohol, the talk steered toward the choice of covering each other, just for the night, in the threadbare blanket of a simple sexual encounter. I had never been seriously tempted, but I had felt truly sorry for many of them. Then, near the end with Donald, I had my own horror story. It wasn't that I didn't know marriages that worked, but I had to agree with Harper: not too many happy people. I conceded with a nod.

"My book's ambition is to point out how, if you understand the correct way to get a job and manage a career, the power of the analogous relationship between *whom you love* and *what you do* becomes synergistic and creates a new you: one who is whole—who is real. Wouldn't it be nice to wake up in the morning and not have to make a distinction between your life and who you pretend to be?"

"Is that how your life is, Harper?"

"This is about you. You need my book, Casey. You need a new career, and you need to stop living without love. The two can be done at one time."

"If you ever write the book."

"I believe I've just started."

CHAPTER ONE

SHOULD YOU LEAVE OR STAY?

Harper asked me if I was okay, and I told him I was fine, no worries. I went home and it felt like the day the divorce was final.

That day I sat at my dining room table without an idea in the world. I don't mean I didn't know where I wanted to live or if I wanted to remarry; I mean I didn't know if I should sit in the dining room or move to the couch, whether I should sleep, eat, or do laundry. Hannah said, "I know you, girl. You saw this coming at some level, and you've got a plan." But I didn't see it coming. And I didn't have a plan.

Today I took two Ambien, chased them with two Oreo cookies, some skim milk, and another Ambien, and opened my arms to oblivion.

In a couple of days I had decided Harper was just being Harper. I didn't think he was lying, but I decided he was taking a few facts, blowing them up, and making a lot of assumptions. My boss had certainly not been acting like he was in any trouble. And how did Harper know that if they did bring in some new honcho he was going to clean house? No, Harper was trying to make a sale and I was just his next placement, wrapped in empathy. And as for his imaginary book being the answer to my work and love problems? Please. Keep the day job, Harper. I went to the monthly staff meeting with the conviction that Harper was to be ignored. Enjoyed, perhaps, but ignored.

My CEO, Michael Tynan, was at the sales meeting; he never comes to sales meetings.

He sat with his arms folded across his chest, and when he interrupted my boss with a short declaration that he had a responsibility to reverse our sales forecasts sooner rather than later, I knew in an instant Harper was right. My boss was toast. We were all toast.

In the next four days, I did what any reasonable person in crisis would do—I blocked it out entirely. Every time I got a call, I was grateful it wasn't Harper. I needed some time to sort through everything, though I knew that was the complete opposite of what my therapist would tell me I should do.

"What would you do if you weren't afraid?" she would lean over and whisper, and I would catch a whiff of the cinnamon Tic Tacs she always chewed but never offered. ("I would ask you why you hoard something that costs less than two dollars and comes sixty to a package.") She was right to call me on it. When I found out about Donald's affair with Sasha, I not only avoided confronting him for a week, I held hands with him at the Met's Picasso exhibit for the first time since we started dating. I fear change even more than humiliation.

I would die before ever admitting this to him, but at times like these I miss Donald. He would stroke my hair while I whined and emoted. He would not try to fix me, but would just nod while I let it all out. Why can't I find the answers without someone touching my hair, and why doesn't it work when I touch it myself?

Sitting at home on a Friday evening, I suddenly realized I could trust Donald to tell me if what I decided to do sounded right. Immediately the idea of trusting Donald cracked me up, and my laughter reverberated through the empty house. My six-year-old Maine Coon, Starbucks, (so named because she turns up at every corner, and is bitter first thing in the morning) ran out of the room, skidding on the hardwood floor like a cartoon tabby.

Then I heard the faint chime of an email arriving, and during the commercial I checked it on my way to the fridge.

Harper Scott. Sent with "high importance." The subject line read:

Harper's Rules: The Recruiter's Guide to Finding a Dream Job and the Right Relationship, by Harper Scott.

My instinct said not to open this now. Not after having two and a half glasses of Kendall Jackson chardonnay that I washed down with eleven Fig Newtons and looking like a raccoon because I had rubbed my mascara the way I do when I'm stressed. My instincts told me I should read this after a good sleep, not when vulnerable.

I believe my instincts; I just tend to ignore them. I went to the living room and sat down to read.

The opening paragraphs were vintage Harper:

Author's Note: Now that you have bought this book, it makes no difference to me if you are trying to solve your relationship problems or your career issues; they are one and the same. You can't have a great relationship if you fail at your career, and the greatest job in the world is worthless without someone who can share the ups and downs with you. I have learned how to fix both simultaneously for my candidates and clients.

But first a disclaimer. This book will be useless if you are the type who whines and moans about what people or circumstances in your life have done to you, but who are actually not interested in change—the type who define themselves by their problems and will continue to do the things they already know don't work. If this sounds like you, please return the book and buy *Dating for Dummies* or *What's My Parachute?* For the rest of you, let's go. None of you are getting any younger.

Despite Harper's signature combination of callousness and acumen, I had to ask myself if I really wanted my life to change. Do I get some sort of pleasure out of being unhappy? No, I don't think I do. I was happiest when I was happy—I just couldn't sustain it. And right now at my job, all I'm trying to decide is whether I should cut and run or try to make it work.

HARPER'S RULES
Should You Leave or Stay?

It takes little thought and even less courage to leave a relationship that is miserable all the time. The problem for most of you reading this is that *you're not miserable all the time; you're only miserable some of the time!* Some of you will say, "but that's life" and decide to stick it out. Great; that's your call. But some of you will be haunted. In a life this short, isn't it possible to be happy nearly all the time—at work and home?

Misery isn't happiness's foe; "good enough" is.

So you need to decide. I will ask you the same questions I would if you were in my office and I was considering representing you to my corporate clients. After you do the homework I'm about to assign, if you decide to stay in your job or relationship, then take change off the table. Accept that, excluding some unforeseen change, you will be where you are for the rest of your life. It's *okay* to be done with seeking. Embrace it.

But stay away from me, just in case what you have is contagious.

Regardless of whether your primary concern is your personal relationship or your career, answer this diagnostic in terms of your job first, and then you'll see the same rules apply to your relationship. You can do it in reverse too, but it's my book, damn it! Do it my way first.

Time-to-Leave Diagnostic

Q1: Why did you buy this book?

Have you bought other books about changing jobs? When someone leaves your company, do you interrogate them to find out where they are going and why? Do you peruse job boards like Monster or Careerbuilder "just for fun?" How often? Do you get calls on your voice mail from headhunters? Do you return them? Do you find yourself unfocused at work? Have you reworked your résumé even though you're not actively looking?

BOTTOM LINE: if you're acting like you're leaving your job, you're leaving your job. It's just a matter of timing and opportunity. Sometimes we do the right things before we've figured out why they're right.

Q2: Can you pass the "if you were unemployed" test?

If you were unemployed and you had the chance to interview for the job you now have, would you? Or would you be more interested in seeing what else was out there?

BOTTOM LINE: If you are staying at your job just because you are already in it, you should leave. Inert objects stay inert, and so will your career. If fear of unemployment is the only reason you stay, you should leave. We all like easy, but it's not the same as fulfilling.

Q3: Was it ever what you really wanted?

If you made a compromise with yourself when you took your job, your chances of being satisfied by it are slight, regardless of how successful you become at it. Did you take it because you needed quick income? Did you get trapped by convenience? Or did you just make a bad judgment? Maybe your boss left or the company got bought, and the dream is no longer present but you are?

BOTTOM LINE: If none of the original reasons why you took the job are still valid, or you settled for less than you were meant to do, your dream will haunt you until you leave.

Q4: Can we write your eulogy right now?

If you stayed where you are for the rest of your career, are you okay with that? Can we write your eulogy? "She took a job in 2008 at age thirty-four and stayed there until she died at her desk in the fall of 2035?" Picture your tombstone with the two dates and the dash in between. Is that okay with you?

BOTTOM LINE: If you know your story is not yet written and at some point you will seek bigger things, you should leave now if an opportunity arises. (Make all big decisions in your life by considering your "eulogy *Cliff's Notes*": If the decision would merit mention in your eulogy, do it. If the decision is one you'd rather people not hear at your funeral, don't do it.)

Q5: Can you pass the Money Aside Test?

If you didn't have your bills and obligations and you weren't the primary income or the single parent, would you still do your job? Is the intrinsic value of the work or the spirit of your co-workers enough to sustain you if you didn't need an income?

BOTTOM LINE: Money is how adults keep score. It counts, but it doesn't keep us happy. If you wouldn't stay at your job if you could put money aside, then you shouldn't stay now.

Q6: How often do you laugh during the day?

Are you a living, breathing, hostile working environment? Do you make annoying, sighing sounds all day? Have your co-workers stopped asking "are you okay?" because they know the answer?

BOTTOM LINE: If you've stopped laughing, quit immediately. Longevity and success is tied to laughter. The average five-year-old laughs 500 times a day; the average thirty-five-year-old laughs fifteen times a day. We lose 485 laughs in thirty years—why? Your career is far too serious a matter to take seriously.

Q7: Do you believe what they tell you at work?

Has your boss or senior management violated your trust? Is there a pattern of being told one thing only to find you were part of the company "spin?" Did a disclosure you made in confidence show up in a press release?

BOTTOM LINE: Everyone lies. It's essential to a civilized society. But there are white lies and there are lies. If you have lost your basic trust in your boss or organization, then you've met an obstacle you cannot overcome. In life and work, love means no reservations.

Q8: Do you love the job but feel uncomfortable in the culture?

Is there a mismatch in the attitudes and values of the people who surround you? Is the way you dress or how you spend your free time making you feel like you don't fit? Do you ever think that if you could change the culture, the job would be great?

BOTTOM LINE: Cultures don't change. You assimilate or you leave. Relationships that work don't require change on a massive scale.

Q9: Are you staying because they "need you right now" and you "can't do that to your colleagues?" Are you disillusioned but held hostage by guilt?

BOTTOM LINE: Get over yourself. The company will not only survive but flourish with someone new who goes at the job happy and hard. If you're going through the motions, then get in motion—out the door.

Q10: Has your body already told you to leave, but you're hard of hearing?

Are you listless? Eating comfort carbs or not eating enough? Are you having trouble sleeping or sleeping too much? Have you lost interest—in everything? Are you self-medicating with drugs, alcohol, or sex? Does your lower back or neck ache every day? Is sarcasm your first line of defense? Are you aware how unattractive all these are? I don't like you already!

BOTTOM LINE: Pain is your body's way of demanding change, and you need to listen. The second you make the decision to leave, you will feel a lifting sensation, and you will start to come back to yourself.

Don't sit there and nod your head and move on! Answer these questions honestly, and you'll get an overarching feeling one way or another. Either your relationship is broken and you should make a change, or you should decide it's better than you thought and you will stay. Do the work and make the call.

I knew I should go to bed, but Harper had stirred things up and now I was wired. Tired, wired, and a little drunk—and I'm going to try and determine whether I should leave my job? Oh hell, why not? I couldn't get Harper's "diagnostics" out of my head, and I found myself drifting from my job back to my courting days with Donald, to that very sweet and false time every couple enjoys.

Was it ever what you wanted?

No, it wasn't. He wanted to take care of me. He seemed like such a good man, and after all the unreliable bad boys who had no aspirations beyond a good time, it seemed like I should be grateful. He wasn't threatened that I made more money than he did. He wasn't funny, but he thought I was funny, which seemed far more important. He was gentle with Starbucks and he not only cooked, he didn't hold it against me that I was helpless without a microwave. Most of all, he was my rock. Nothing could rattle him.

But I never believed it was forever. I would often imagine being with someone else who was spontaneous, who had a mind so fast I could barely keep up, who made me tingle when I touched him. I didn't want Donald to leave, but I didn't want him, either. When I turned thirty and he started to talk about kids, I would change the subject. I would set goals we had to reach before we got pregnant: pay our mortgage down, get the regional sales manager's job. I urged him to get his Master's degree. I was willing to make him seem inadequate so I could avoid the reality that he was not the love of my life.

And I never told him; only Hannah knew. When we were in the limousine going to the church on the day of my wedding, she popped champagne, poured us each a glass, and recited our secret toast: "Here's to Donald; he'll be a great first husband."

Can you pass the "if you were unemployed" test?

This one was easy. I was one of SAP's top producers. I was happy—apparently unlike Sasha, the wife of Kevin, our inside sales director; she began sleeping with Donald a few weeks after I introduced them at our company summer bash. I even told Donald to let her play on his side of the volleyball net. I still remember the look on her face when they high fived after a nasty spike. I think the affair started that instant, no matter when it was consummated. SAP was the big time, the Show. I'm in my prime but back in the minors.

So, you bet if I were unemployed I'd interview again.

And, I suddenly realized, if I hadn't married Donald and I had a chance to date him exclusively or date others as well, I would date others. I would not settle again.

Now I see what Harper is getting at. When you're deciding whether to stay at a job or in a relationship, it's the same qualifying procedure. I put on a pot of coffee.

If you're acting like you're leaving, you're leaving.

When Harper first recruited me, the first thing he said to me was, "I identified myself as a headhunter. Why did you return the call?"

"Come on, Harper, haven't you ever been tempted?"

"Personally or professionally?"

"Either." You want to flirt, bring it.

"Personally I'm tempted this very second," he said. "Professionally, never. I do what I'm meant to do. There is no variance between whom I show you and who I am. I make more money than I am able to spend, try though I may, so I am absolutely safe from someone like me."

"And at what point do you think you could get over yourself a little?"

"That's to be determined. Casey, you should have the same goal: to be unrecruitable. But you're not. There's something missing. You sense I could help, and you're right. I can."

"And yet, personally, you said you're tempted right now. What are we to make of that?"

"Only that you're fabulous."

"Apparently not fabulous enough."

"I love my wife. We have a deal, and I honor the terms. Mutual trust."

If you've lost basic trust . . . you've met an obstacle you cannot overcome.

It was suddenly so clear to me. I wanted to be in relationships where I could trust completely and safely: to live, as Harper said, *without reservation*. But in order to trust you must be trustworthy, and so far in my thirty-four years—well, thirty-five in four months and thirteen days—I couldn't say I had been. I'd been waiting for something better to come along without letting go of whatever stability I had at the time. It was wrong, and I have paid my dues. So why did I feel so loose, so light?

I stood up and paced the room. I wanted to go for a run; I suddenly wanted to kiss someone. I was flooded with hope, as if a syringe full of it were injected straight into my heart. I, having proudly refused alimony, was alone in the world save for a churlish cat. Despite these facts—or because of them—I felt completely in control and sorry for all human beings who were not me.

If you're acting like you're leaving a relationship, you're leaving the relationship.

I get it, Harper, and I now know what I need to do: I am going to quit my job without having a new one! Hurry up Monday, you're holding a good woman back!

CHAPTER TWO

HOW TO RESIGN FROM A JOB OR END A RELATIONSHIP

The following Monday I was heading into the office, eager for battle. How does your personal music know what is going on in your life? I remember sitting in a terminal in St. Louis listening to my iPod as I went through my mail. Just as I opened the papers Donald's lawyer had prepared, Bonnie Raitt's "I Can't Make You Love Me if You Don't" came on, and I cried so hard I had to hide in a stall in the ladies' room. Now, Bachman-Turner Overdrive's "Takin' Care of Business" was playing on the classic rock station while I was on my way to quit my job. Just to keep from jinxing it, I turned off the sound system.

The moment I sat at my desk, I took a deep breath and called my boss. I told him I needed to see him as soon as possible about a serious and sensitive matter that could not wait.

I decided to let Harper know. I opted for a text message. "I am giving my notice in less than an hour. I appreciated your email last night, sorry, your 'book.' Try not to gloat. FYI."

Three minutes later my direct line buzzed: Harper's number.

"Did you do it yet?"

"No, in a few minutes. Why?"

"Because you're not going to. That's why."

"Why not?"

"Because you'd be breaking one of the cardinal rules:

Harper's Rule: You don't quit a job until you have another job.

"It's like a commandment. How could you not know that?"

"Why didn't you put that in the chapter?"

"Because it's in the next chapter!"

"And why didn't you send it to me?"

"Because I haven't written it yet."

"Oh, for the love of God, Harper. He's going to be here any minute. I demanded the meeting; I told him it was serious and sensitive."

"Okay, no problem. There are many things you might need to talk to your boss about that are serious and sensitive. Tell him you need time off for elective surgery. Tell him you've decided to adopt a child and you may need to go to Guatemala..."

"Harper, your casual lying really scares me."

"But I'm making up lies for *you* to tell. And there's nothing casual about it."

"You told me I was marketable. Why would another company hold it against me that I'm unemployed?"

"Because that's how it works. Hold on. I'm driving in, and I'm going to pull over before I get killed. I can't shift and talk with my hands at the same time...

"Listen to me. You can't give notice. You'll lose all your leverage. It's not fair, but that's how it is. Companies believe good people are never out of a job. So if you're unemployed, then how good could you be? And the longer you're out, the worse it gets."

"So then what, Harper, I have to play a game? I have to live a lie in order to get a great job?"

"Now you've got it! And, by the way, doing it my way, you continue to get paid. Your way, you start living off savings."

I knew Harper was trying to look out for me, and I knew he was probably right. So how come so often doing the right thing can make you feel so crummy inside?

"What about your book, Harper? With your logic, no one should ever leave a marriage without having another partner to go to first. You are saying no one will want me now that I'm single and available, that I should have found someone else while I was still married because I was more attractive then."

"You want to play hardball, Casey? The answer is yes: We want what others have, not what they discard."

"I seduce the best people from companies and offer their direct competitors a chance to steal them away. That is the thrill of it, the magic. It's why they pay me. And yes, the principle holds for relationships. You can be mortified if you want, but the fact is: Most people don't have the courage to end a marriage—or a job—until they are motivated by the prospect of going to someone else."

"You should know this better than anyone. Donald sure did."

I felt a stinging in my scalp, the way you do when you first step into a really cold shower.

I've only seen Donald once since the divorce ended. It was by chance at a mall during Christmas time. We hugged stiffly, and as we pulled back, I noticed the Victoria's Secret bag, and he noticed me noticing and shrugged, and we both laughed so hard we had to sit on the bench outside of Banana Republic.

"I hate you, Harper Scott. I don't think we should speak again."

"That was a cheap shot. I'm sorry. I was just trying to keep you from making a mistake."

"I'm quitting my job this morning, Harper. End of story. I think your theory about relationships and jobs does in fact hold; you're just wrong as to how. I'm not going to deceive my company. I don't want to take their money when I'm no longer committed. And I don't want to work for any company that doesn't respect me for that. And if I am ever again in a relationship that stops working, I am going to be honest, make a break, and free myself to look for someone else. And any guy that doesn't respect me for that—I don't want him, either."

"Okay, I'm in," Harper said. "Take good notes because I'm about to dictate Part Two to you right now. Here's how to give notice and end a relationship. Ready?"

It was too late. My boss knocked once and then bounded right into my office. Harper was all over it in an instant. "Say goodbye and act like you're hanging up, but leave your speaker on."

He quietly told me to pay attention to the screen because he was going to walk me through this via instant messaging, and he suggested I keep my mouse within easy reach. He told me to relax and trust him. "Now hang up, Casey."

"Okay, well, I have to go now," I said, and managed to activate my speaker while hanging up my handset.

I suddenly felt like I was the flight attendant and both pilots were passed out; Harper was ground control assuring me that anyone could land a commercial airliner and that we were not all going to die.

Within a few moments, while my boss and I did the obligatory warm-up, Harper's first IM came across my screen:

HARPER'S RULES
How to Terminate a Relationship

Rule #1: Use direct, simple language.

Deliver the bad news within one sentence. Don't say "I think," don't say "I don't know how to say this," and definitely don't say "I want you to know this is hard for me and that it's not about you."

My boss was still going on about his daughter's award-winning crab cakes at the culinary institute she was attending when I blurted out, "I'm resigning. I'm sorry to interrupt, I'm sure they were fabulous crab cakes, but I want you to know I quit."

Rule #2: Realize this is not an exit interview.

This is not the time to tell him all that went wrong.

On cue, my boss said he was shocked. He asked why I had come to such a decision. I stammered something out about how much I appreciated his mentoring, but this was just a gut feeling I had. "Okay, that sucked. Do I need to script this for you? He is about to ask you what he can do to get you to stay. Here is what you tell him . . ."

As I was trying to read Harper's message, my boss said, "But your gut feeling must have come from somewhere. Is it about money? I have a lot of flexibility, Casey."

"Repeat this, word for word:"

There are two kinds of breakups: the kind where you don't really want to break up but you're trying to change someone's behavior, and the kind where you just want out. I just want out.

And out it came, word for word. It hit him hard. I realized he knew that the word was out, that Tynan had given up on him. "Far be it from me to try to change a woman's mind. I've had two wives and three daughters, and I haven't been able to do it yet. We'll miss you," he said, to which Harper replied, "Oh, gag me. Okay, you're doing great."

Rule #3: Never burn a bridge.

Offer two week's notice. Tell him you will work hard during that two weeks, and you will not disparage the company.

Rule #4: Ask for a written reference and a commitment to give you verbal references on demand.

My boss was more than happy to commit to the reference, and when he said he would tell any VPs of sales that they'd be "foolish not to hire you," I looked over at my screen: "Excellent. You're done. End this meeting. Don't let it go on because he'll try to dig for ways to get you to reconsider."

Sure enough, ten minutes later, my boss was still in his chair, but Harper bailed me out.

Rule #5: Offer to submit, just for documentation's purposes, a written letter of resignation.

When I made the offer, my boss nodded and then almost whispered, "Can I ask you one more question, Casey? Can I have the name of your headhunter?"

"He's a loser," Harper wrote. "Tell him you'll email the contact info, and I'll give you the name of another headhunter who is as big a loser. They'll love each other."

I placed my hand on my boss's hand and quietly and stoically said, "Of course. His name is Harper Scott."

CHAPTER THREE

AND NOW THE COUNTEROFFER

The morning after I quit my job, I could find no reason not to go to my gym.

I've been a member of Gold's Gym for three years, and each month they take one hundred and twenty-nine dollars from me, despite the fact that I don't go for months at a time. But I never quit the gym. Knowing they are taking my money every month regardless of my lack of presence is what gives me hope that someday I'll be able to sustain an interest long enough to make it a habit. So here I am again, everyone!

Ten minutes into my ride on the elliptical, my cell phone rang.

"Hi, Harper," I managed, my breath labored.

"Just because you're unemployed, you don't have to take my call during sex."

I explained where he had caught me. "I have two goals, Harper: get a job and lose weight. Of course if I don't get a job, I'll lose weight because I won't be able to buy food. What's up?"

"Tynan is going to ask you to have dinner, and then he's going to hit you with a counteroffer. Lots more money, probably your boss's job."

"So what do I do? I have to hear him out, right? I can't insult him and not go to dinner. I mean, I need him for a reference, too."

Harper laughed. "By tonight I will have sent you chapter three. It will walk you through how to handle the counteroffer."

My concentration was broken by Cute Guy, a Gold's employee, now on the glider next to me. He was pointing to the control panel.

"Sorry," Cute Guy said, "I know you're on the phone, but did you know your machine is off? You've been riding with no resistance." I could hear Harper crack up.

"Oh. Thanks. Would it do any good to pretend I knew that?" And Cute Guy flashed a really great, genuine smile.

"I can tell you're having a moment. You should have the pages by early evening."

"Okay, thanks," I said. "Does this make me your muse, Harper?"

"Not in the least. I've been thinking about this book forever."

When I got home, there was already an email from Harper:

Your homework assignment before you get tonight's chapter. Answer this question: "Did you ever consider going back to Donald?"

That could wait; it was only my first day unemployed, and you have to pace yourself.

I was about to fade into a nap when the phone rang. Tynan's secretary asked me to meet him the following evening at a restaurant that required a month's lead for a reservation. Suddenly I was wide awake, Harper's question seared into my brain.

Did you ever consider going back to Donald?

Yes, Harper, I did.

When you get divorced in your thirties, and there are no children, and you've only been together a half dozen years, you walk out of the courtroom thinking you may never see your former spouse ever again. You imagine one day reading in the obituaries that your ex has died, and the accompanying sidebar points out trenchantly how he never recovered emotionally from his failed marriage and that he died of heartbreak, penniless and alone, survived only by his ex, who lived a full and remarkable life and is now living in a beach house on the ocean, and I mean right *on* the ocean.

It was not in the plan to get a call from Donald four months after the divorce was final, especially since he was crying so hard it took me a moment to realize it was him. Big Gerry, as we all referred to his dad, had died that morning. Big Gerry was the kindest man I ever knew. He called me the night Donald moved out to tell me his son was a fool and that he loved me very much.

Donald said he was sorry to bother me but he thought I should know. Then he hung up. I drove to his condo, knocked twice, and opened the door, momentarily thinking this was inappropriate and that Sasha would be furious. I calmed him down and made him tea. I told him what I felt at the time, what I still feel: that all that was good and sweet and endearing about Big Gerry was true of Donald as well. I asked him if there were arrangements he wanted me to make. He said all he wanted was for me to stay a while. We made a meal, we opened wine, and we recounted stories to soothe the pain.

When he mentioned that Sasha was at a family reunion in Sacramento and wasn't coming back for the funeral, I nodded and agreed it was a long flight. And I spent the night. We went to separate bedrooms to play the dance out, but he knocked on the door within a few minutes, he walked toward the bed, and I opened my arms. I knew that I was helping him cheat on Sasha, but all I could think was that I deserved this after all I had been through.

When I woke up, I heard the familiar sound of ESPN's SportsCenter. When Donald moved out, my first act of independence was to get rid of the wall-mounted flat screen Sony in the bedroom and to promise myself to never again sleep with a man who watches sports before bed. And yet the sound was oddly comforting. Donald was already halfway through a bowl of oatmeal. He smiled and handed me a bowl of my own, along with a steaming cup of coffee. This was our morning ritual for our entire marriage. How did we get back here so easily?

"I cooked it. In a pan. No microwave."

"I'll alert the Food Channel."

We ate in silence. He kissed my shoulder. And then out it came.

"Let's stay together through the funeral. It's just a couple of days. I'll pack some stuff and follow you home. Okay?"

"You want to play house?" I asked. And he looked down, as Donald always did when he was gathering himself. And when he looked back up his eyes were wet. He shrugged. And my response came out of me from someplace deep inside, someplace I thought was gone.

"Okay."

Suddenly I realized the doorbell was ringing. I shook off the groggy nostalgia and found a manila envelope on the ground with a note from Harper.

"You absolutely cannot go to dinner with Tynan without reading what's inside."

I tore open the envelope and saw the cover page: "Harper's Rules: Why You Never Accept a Counteroffer."

But I wasn't ready for Harper's propaganda. I put it down on the dining room table and went upstairs. As I transferred a load of whites from washer to dryer, I found myself drifting back to the week of Big Gerry's funeral, my after-the-fact performance as Donald's wife.

The funeral itself was the easy part. I'm cool in a crisis; I think clearly under extreme pressure. As I brought drinks and plates of potato salad to various mourners, as I tipped the hearse driver because no one in the family remembered, I thought for a moment that the real problem in my life is not crisis management, but all that time in between crises, when none of my choices seem as sure or righteous. I realized that sitting in Big Gerry's living room on the day of his funeral was the most contentment I had felt in a long time.

That night we decided to forego cooking and drive into the city to get sushi. We drank way too much sake. Donald told me how much it surprised him to miss Starbucks and the way she would climb on his chest at night and suckle his neck. Donald started to slur his words a little.

"You want me to drive home?" I asked.

"Where is home, Casey?"

"Sorry—my house."

"I want it to be 'our house' again," he croaked. "Maybe this . . . is why he died. Maybe it was to get it through our thick skulls that we have to be together."

I touched his cheek. "He died because he died, Donny. It had nothing to do with us. And what about Sasha? You love Sasha. You threw your world away for her. You had to do that for a reason."

"Let's go home," he said. "We'll work it out."

We didn't last the night. When we walked in the house, Donald nearly let Starbucks out. This is one of my hot buttons and one of my few house rules. Starbucks has never gone outside. Neighbors warned us from day one that there were coyotes in the woods nearby. Donald closed the door just in time, and I tried to tell myself he was out of practice, but the thought occurred: nothing will change if we get back together. He will let Starbucks out one day and I will lose her, and it will be just punishment for not being strong enough to move on.

There were two voice mails on my machine when we got home. The first was Hannah inviting me to a farmer's market in New Milford on Saturday, and the second, to my surprise and Donald's shock, was Sasha.

"Hi, Casey, it's Sasha Kiernan. I'm sorry to bother you at home, but I've been trying to get in touch with Donald. I've talked to his mom, and she said you left together. This is weird for me to call you, but he hasn't called me back."

You'll never trust him again. You will live your life looking over your shoulder. You will never be able to love this man without reservation again.

"What is your actual status with Sasha?" I said.

"Technically, we're engaged."

"Technically?"

"She has a ring on her finger."

"If we got back together a year from now, all the things that drove us apart would return. You know that, right?"

"Maybe," he said. He looked away from me. It was time to wrap this up. I smiled at him, a big friendly smile.

"We don't love each other, Donny. We have a divorce decree that proves it. We love what we used to be for a short time, a long time ago. When we get scared, it's easier to go back to what we know."

I didn't know when or if I would ever see him again, but I felt at peace with either outcome. I had always heard change brought growth, that it was necessary. I never knew it could bring peace.

The flashback ended when I woke up and realized I had not only fallen asleep on my bed covered with laundry, but had drooled all over a pair of clean khakis. I felt rejuvenated by the memory, and I knew what I had to do. I called Tynan.

"Hi. I'm going to respect your time and avoid all the small talk. I'm not coming to dinner tomorrow night."

"Has something come up? We can reschedule."

"No, I am tragically available. But you don't want to have dinner with me. If you did, it would have happened sometime in the eighteen months I've been working for you. You want to convince me to stay and make me a counteroffer, but I don't want to waste your energy or time."

"I see. I'd appreciate you paying me the respect of hearing me out."

Spoken like a man used to getting what he wanted. And the way he said it made me feel unreasonable and feckless. But I knew it was a tactic and that a tactic was all it was.

"I'm not going to stay. Not if you make me VP of sales, not if you double my salary or fully vest my equity. Still want to pick up the check for a fancy dinner? If you do, I'm game; I've got nothing in the fridge."

He laughed, though I could tell he didn't want to. He got to where he was by knowing when to walk away. He said he admired my "spunk" and would try to find another guest for dinner.

When I hung up, I felt the same peace as when Donald drove off on the night of Big Gerry's funeral.

Later that night I walked by the dining room table, saw the envelope sent by Harper, and realized I hadn't read it.

HARPER'S RULES
Why You Should Never Accept a Counteroffer

1. Why did you have to resign in order to get the counteroffer? Why weren't you worth it before?
2. Where did the money come from? Is it your next raise early?
3. Your loyalty will always be in question.
4. Your company will exact revenge by promoting someone else.
5. The feelings that made you want to leave will return once the heat of the moment passes.
6. You will regret lacking the courage to make the change you knew was best for your career.
7. Once trust is broken, it cannot be repaired. Nothing will ever be the same.

Well, well, Harper my friend. Nothing personal, but I figured this all out by myself. Harper was right, though: counteroffers, be they from a self-involved CEO or a heart-sick ex-husband, are the same dangerous proposition.

I suppose I should have called Harper to let him know my decision and to thank him for sending the manuscript, but I didn't want him taking credit for me coming to terms with things myself. So when he called the next night, I realized he probably thought I caved and went to dinner.

"Hi. Before you freak out, I didn't go to dinner with Tynan. I cancelled."

"First of all, I do not freak out. Ever. Second, I know you're not at dinner."

"How?"

"Because I'm at dinner with Tynan."

"Excuse me? Did he invite you to meet with me, and you never told me?"

"Chill, please. I would never not tell you something like that. What I would do, though, since you weren't good enough to tell me you cancelled, is show up so I could meet you in the parking lot and talk you out of it, or alternatively, walk you through your responses using sign language from across the room."

"I don't read sign language."

"Me either. I was pleased to see you weren't at his table. I'm proud of you."

"I worked through it. Thanks for your help. But now I feel terrible. He was by himself?"

"No, he's got a couple of lackeys here too. I realized you weren't coming, so I walked over, claimed to be sitting in the bar, and knew that he'd invite me. The appetizers were phenomenal, by the way."

"Is there any shame in your body?"

"Not a trace."

"I need to ask you something, Harper. I get all the reasoning behind the dangers of counteroffers, personal or professional. But isn't there ever a time when they work out?"

"Sure. I call them 'Preemptive Counteroffers.' Before leaving any job or person that you once really loved, you go to them preemptively, before quitting or separating, and you explain why you are unhappy, what you need changed. No threat, no blackmail. If they come back to you with an offer preemptively, then they have done so because they are sorry, and it's often right to stay. Make sense?"

"Yes. That's never happened to me in any sense, so I guess it's only right that I'm alone and unemployed."

"It's right for now, baby, but not for long. It's a simple rule:

"Relationships are to be enjoyed, not endured.

"I have to let you go; here come the entrees. My steak looks fantastic."

CHAPTER FOUR

GETTING BACK OUT THERE— RÉSUMÉS AND NETWORKING

I sat in a diner in Bridgeport that made Denny's look like a Ritz Carlton. It was 9 A.M., and I hurried into the place after making sure twice that my car was locked. I nursed three cups of coffee, but Harper never showed. I texted him, emailed him, and having had enough, I dialed his direct line.

"Where are you? Brunch this is not," I hissed.

"Sorry, going to be a no-show. You never sent me a new résumé, and I don't think you're ready," Harper said in a maddeningly calm voice.

"How am I not ready?"

"You still feel sorry for yourself."

"Harper, you have my old résumé. You know my background. Get me a job like the one I had, with a better company for more money. Do I have to tell you how this works?"

"Any headhunter can take you from one rut and put you in another rut. This is your chance to decide what you want, and to not settle."

For the seventh time in an hour, the waitress asked me if I was ready to order, and I succumbed to the pressure and asked for an egg white omelet with no cheese and no home fries. She gave me a look that said she had no respect for anyone who couldn't handle cheese.

"Hey, you know what, I'm not going to discuss this with you when you make me drive nearly an hour on the Merritt Parkway during rush hour to meet you at this sad excuse for a restaurant and then don't show." I lowered my voice and looked around. "Do you know what types of characters are here?"

"The characters, as you call them, are mostly hourly workers from Sikorsky Aircraft, the painting division. Probably not a woman in the place other than Chaz, who just took your order. All guys coming home from the midnight shift. The first shift started hours ago. They dip blades and vanes, after they've been milled and polished, into a vat of paint, and they hang them on hooks and roll them into ovens. When they open the doors to the ovens, a blast of heat hits them that makes them puke until they get used to it."

"How do you know all that?"

"I worked at that diner for four summers while I went to Yale. Look into the kitchen, Casey. You can see it from the counter. Tell me what you see."

There were two Hispanic men with bandanas on their foreheads. One of them had a ponytail. They were moving rapidly from the grill, jammed with small pools of eggs and link sausages and crackling bacon, to the toaster and to the fryer. One man sprinkled mushrooms into the pool of eggs. Their bodies and the frenetic tempo of their movements made them look young, but when one turned toward me to bring a plate to the counter, his brow was dripping with sweat, his eyes darkly circled. He might have been much older. For a second he paused and wiped his face with his apron, and I wondered if he would take off the white apron and walk out the door. But he didn't. He punched his friend playfully on the shoulder, grabbed a couple of eggs from the glass bowl near the grill, and started over.

Harper never said a word. I wanted to yell at him that if I can't ever feel sorry for myself because someone else in the world is suffering more than I am, I will never be able to feel sorry for myself, and who can live like that? But it was suddenly very clear: I have been so blessed and have become so spoiled.

"Okay, Harper, I get it."

My meal arrived, and suddenly I realized I was famished. I smiled broadly at Chaz and waved my fork in gratitude at one of my cooks. He put one hand on his stomach, one hand on his lower back, and bowed formally, grinning all the while.

"You never intended to meet me here this morning, did you, Harper?"

"No."

"You know, Harper, I always assumed you were a rich kid. I guess because of Yale."

"Look above the cash register, third picture down. The baseball player is Carl Yastrzemski of the Red Sox. The guy with his arm around him mugging in the picture is my dad. The kid between them is me."

I could see no trace of my Harper in the grainy, wide smile of the little boy. But I could see a lot of him in his father.

"Is he still alive?"

"Yastrzemski? Far as I know."

"I meant your dad."

"I know."

I waited. But there was no more.

"Well," I rallied, "it's a great picture. I'm glad to report that it's still here. And I guess I'm glad I'm here. Do you ever come back?"

"Breakfast yesterday, kiddo. The only way to safeguard where you're going is by not forgetting where you come from. You and I don't have real jobs, Casey. Look around you. Those people have real jobs."

He hung up, and I thought for a moment of all the motivational seminars I'd been to over the years. Robbins, Covey, Dr. Phil . . . I knew Harper would never go to a self-help seminar. He didn't need to; he had his diner.

But he also has his job and an income. I could run out of money, and I can't seem to face it. My money issues are exposing, well . . . my issues with money.

Salespeople know a lot about *making* money. But what I couldn't admit to Harper, what I have never admitted to anyone, is that I am terrible *with* money. I can muster no interest in my own finances, I understand almost nothing about taxes and investment strategies, and I willingly delegated all of these concerns to Donald. We had a silent pact: I never told anyone how little he earned in relation to me, and he never told anyone that I didn't balance the checkbook, had no concept of a budget, and had no idea exactly where our money was kept.

The divorce exposed me. When my lawyer handed me the financial disclosure form where Donald had listed various mutual funds, bonds, and 401(k) statements, I had no way of knowing if the totals were correct. Was this the right amount in the checking account? Was this CD for 15K that is only in his name a clandestine account or did I know about it? Did I want Donald to buy me out of the house and at what price? No clue. But I knew Donald would be fair.

I stood in the doorway of my den and looked at the mountain of papers on the desk. Before Donald became extinct, the office desk was Finance Central, and all our personal papers and records were in their various drawers. The day he moved out he walked me through the system like a tour guide at the Met, eager to see my gasps of awe. And now, nearly two years later, the papers and bills have revolted.

Please understand: my walk-in closet is organized by color, season, and designer. I could find you a presentation folder I used for a product I no longer sell for a company I no longer work for, and I could recite the notes by heart. I always thought this meant chaos had no place in my world for the things that matter, but it turns out just the opposite is true. I tolerate chaos in the things that matter most because then I can blame the chaos and ignore the fear that created it. Taking care of our money was something I didn't want to do and Donald did. But I would, often cruelly, make it clear to Donald that what I did was the heavy lifting—making the money—and he was an underachieving bean counter. Our friends all wonder how I cannot hate Donald when he left me for another woman in such a humiliating fashion. But they weren't there for the daily humiliations he endured. If someone were keeping score, it would still not even be close.

I decided to accept the fact that I might always be alone, that no one is coming to rescue me, that it was time to act. I plugged in the shredder, and started working my way through the pile. It was a joke.

I am unemployed; why do I need a housekeeper every two weeks? She's gone. I can clean my own house. (I can feel myself regretting this already . . . the deep clean in the toilets? Eww! How far the mighty fall.)

The $200 haircut from fabulous Simon that I drive all the way into the East Village for is on hold until I get a job.

Why do I still have a landline? I can live with just my cell phone. Of course sometimes the signal is weak . . . NO! Cancel the landline; we are taking order back in this damn house!

Starbucks can go without the high-priced organic food and just eat Fancy Feast like every other damn cat! On cue, she jumped on the table and rubbed her head against my face. Oh fine, you get your damn IAMS, but no landline!

For the first time in my adult life, I added up my monthly expenses. I have not only not cut down on my spending, but with my added time off, I have been doing *more* shopping. I have been in such denial.

I took a respite from my pile of gloom and went to Google. I put in the phrase: how much an unemployed person should have in savings. I had 14,000 results to choose from, and they all said the same thing: at least six months of living expenses.

Okay, if I am employed in the next two months, I will not have to break into CDs or (gulp) my 401(k). And I will cheerfully kill myself before asking my father for money, but I am squandering my severance, and the scary truth is, at first, I turned down the severance package. I told them I didn't need it.

Because I would be the primary money earner in our marriage, Donald offered to sign a prenuptial agreement. Gracious, right?

However, I am a romantic. To me, if you have a pre nup, you are saying the marriage will fail. I couldn't sign a pre nup and then stand before God and make vows about forever. I called Donald and said I wanted no part of a pre nup.

I took the same attitude with my career. To talk about severance was to admit failure before we attempted to succeed. Severance was as unromantic as alimony!

When I first worked with Harper, I told him I didn't approve of severance.

"Nonsense, baby girl. I will get you a severance, and you will take it cheerfully."

"I have certain principles, Harper, and you represent me."

"It's an idiotic principle, and I won't allow it."

"Do you have a pre nup, Harper?"

"Yes."

"Of course you do. Do you have a severance at work as well? Even though you keep telling me you are the top headhunter in creation, and everyone tries to hire you day and night?"

"That is an exaggeration, though slight, and you bet I have a severance, one much better than I can get for you."

"Why?"

He lowered his voice, and I could hear him almost grit his teeth.

"Because, Casey, I am not the person I was ten years ago, and I will not be the person I am now in ten years. And neither will my boss or my wife. I cannot predict circumstances or changes of heart, and for you to think you can makes you incredibly and unbearably arrogant. It is an insult to God."

"To God?! So the one time I ever hear you make a spiritual reference is when we are talking about separation agreements in a comp plan?"

"You want spiritual references? Meet me at St. Mary's on Farmington Ave at 7:30 this Sunday. Haven't missed a mass in years. You?"

That was a low blow. I was on airplanes all week. Of course, since I left my job I still continue to sleep in on Sundays. I had no idea how much fatigue not working can create. There is no rest for the unweary.

"Okay, here's spiritual: I think accepting a severance is bad karma, Harper. It makes me feel like I'm creating a bad end for myself. I know that sounds crazy to you."

"No. It sounds young." And then, for the first time, he called me by the nickname he would use in the years that have followed.

"Look, kiddo, things end." He sounded far away when he said it.

"Businesses go bankrupt, the fastest guy blows out a knee, the sweetest little boy becomes the meanest teenager, jobs get eliminated, you fall out of love, and parents and friends die. Things end, kiddo."

"Don't they preach cheery thoughts over at St. Mary's?"

"Severance is sacred. Non-negotiable."

"I can tell. Okay. I will defer to your judgment."

Now that I am living off my severance, thank God I listened. Not that I will ever admit that to Harper.

I opened the bottom right drawer of the big oak desk, and in my "Harper" file was his severance email from my first job. He was writing "Harper's Rules" even then.

HARPER'S RULES
Severance Made Simple

1. Duration. A standard severance is one week's pay for every year you served the company. If you leave in the first two years, for any reason, you automatically get two weeks' pay.
2. Vacation/Personal Time. You also receive monies equivalent to all the vacation time, personal days, and sick days you had accrued.
3. Health Benefits. Your health benefits stay intact and are paid by the company throughout the duration of the severance. After the severance has lapsed, you have the option of carrying your benefits yourself via a COBRA plan for eighteen additional months.
4. Still on Payroll. For purposes of outside inquiry, references, customers, or vendors, you are on the payroll. You will retain a voice mail and email account, and you will not be removed from the company website nor will any announcement be made of you leaving the company until the severance period is up.
5. References. The company will provide written references for future employers, to be reviewed and approved by the separated employee. (We may need to negotiate this if you leave in someone's bad graces or if you just plain do a bad job. My advice? Do neither.)
6. Outplacement services. The company will provide, at its expense, access to résumé writing services, printing services, phone and Internet, and admin support. This includes an office or workspace. Third-party outplacement service fees will be available at the employee's discretion, to a maximum of 10K.
7. Bonuses/incentives. All profit bonuses and/or performance bonuses that would have been paid in the calendar year of the severance period will be paid by the end of the severance period.
8. No Retro Payback. The employee will not be asked to return or reimburse any sign-on bonuses, merit bonus, or contest or incentive prizes, such as trips or meals. This includes relocation expenses at the time of hire.
9. Company car. The employee will have the option of buying the provided vehicle or returning it.
10. Equity. If equity earned is fully vested, the employee may cash out or may choose to stay an investor in the company.

11. Tuition. If the employee has begun classes under a tuition reimbursement program, the company will pay for the classes in full.

I had to smile at Harper's postscript. "PS: I know the company car is a Camry, and you wouldn't be caught dead driving one. Work with me here!"

I put the "Harper" file away and remembered how scared I used to be that Donald might find it. Harper flirted in email, and I wondered if any of the clippings I had printed out and attached had any of my replies included.

I felt guilty and a little dirty, though I had never even so much as touched Harper. Whenever he was on the phone, Donald would refer to him as "your buddy." There was never any other discussion of the matter until the very end, when my humiliation had become public, and I was asking Donald how he could sleep with another woman in our bed.

"Go ahead," Donald snarled, "make me out to be a monster. You can't make me feel any worse than I do, but take away the sex, and the only difference between Sasha and Harper is a matter of degree. It's the same intention."

Had we signed a divorce agreement during that period, I would have demanded things I really didn't care about just to hurt Donald. In fact, Connecticut has a ninety-day grace period after you file for divorce precisely to let everyone cool down. We were the better for it, but there is no such grace period at work. Companies should take a page from the dissolution of marriages and institute a "no fault" rule, where no one can quit or fire anyone for ninety days, until everyone has cooled down.

But Harper would say that is idealistic and not going to happen. In the meantime, we need severance agreements.

CHAPTER FIVE

THE TRUTH ABOUT RÉSUMÉS

When you're unemployed you find out that the day, which was impossibly short for everything you were trying to cram into it before, actually creeps by. You start wondering why more housewives haven't written screenplays and what is taking so long to cure cancer. However, despite the increased amount of time, you still get almost nothing done.

So as I summoned the energy to sit down to write my résumé, with Harper's help, (after the diner visit, he anointed me as ready) the phone rang, and I remembered: telemarketing calls come in all day long. If you don't pick up, they don't leave messages, so I had no idea this was happening when I was working or when Donald and I were both gone all day. Lately a tenacious salesperson, one Peter Bonetti, had called every day at various times and had even left a couple of messages, but while I respected his salesmanship, I would just delete the message without listening to it. After all, I had a résumé to write.

HARPER'S RULES
Résumés

There are two kinds of candidates. The first kind has a great background that I can bring to market but has a terrible résumé. These candidates think it's impossible to fairly encapsulate their vast life's work in such a short form. They hate their résumés. The second kind has the opposite problem. They believe that had Moses an eleventh tablet, it would have been their résumé. When they first sit down, they take the sacred text from their briefcases, handling it like an ancient scroll or a treasure map. Often the first thing this type of candidate will say to me is, "So, what did you think of my résumé?" as if it were a grandchild or a protégé. This kind of candidate will turn down a tremendous job offer if they feel "it won't look good on my résumé." Such reasoning is the equivalent of a man saying he would be happy to marry his beloved, except it would look bad later to be referred to as someone's "ex-husband."

All of my fellow headhunters will be thrilled when the résumé, which is on the endangered species list, breathes its last. Technically, it is already extinct. Video résumés will be the standard. Some companies already offer the service.

But for now, and for the near term, you need a résumé. No résumé, no interview; you are removed from serious consideration because you're either a prima donna or not serious about making a move. It is one of the first red flags to a headhunter that you are a "shopper."

Understand: To date, *I have never placed a résumé!* But I have also never secured a first meeting for a real job at a major corporation without submitting a résumé, dossier, curriculum vitae, call it what you will. It's a must have. And it must be good! If it's not of a certain quality, make no mistake, they will discard you. Here's the truth about the "system" of reviewing résumés: *Companies want to screen OUT, not screen IN.* So if something small is wrong, you don't get the benefit of the doubt, you get screened. You lose. Got it?

So let's not let that happen.

Your résumé is an advertisement; it is not an affidavit.

We're not selling your memoir here. We're not going to include anything that's not true, but we're sure going to leave out some stuff that is.

Your résumé is a highlight film; it's SportsCenter, not the unedited game footage.

We have between five and fifteen seconds to catch your reader's attention before they either engage or pass. We're going to compress, assuming everyone you send your résumé to has Adult Attention Deficit Disorder.

If God had a résumé, it would be one page.

I know, I know: you've done so much, you have awards, you have honors, you have so many years of excellence. Wake up! Nobody reads the second page. Nobody cares about anything in your background older than ten years back (unless you're 25–35 years old). No one cares how you were *formed*; they care about what you bring to bear in the job they're trying to fill and whether you are qualified. Remember, the purpose of the résumé is to *get an interview.* Period.

Harper's cynical side, always present at the cellular level, seemed to metastasize when it came to résumés. But then I remembered cruising Monster yesterday just to get a look at some sample résumés and going brain dead within a few moments.

Besides, when Harper gets cynical, I sort of love him, the way you love to see gorillas stretch at the zoo. You want to hug them, even though you know they could crush you.

The phone rang. The name on the screen was Peter Bonetti. God bless you, buddy. Whoever you work for ought to promote you for sheer tenacity. I hit the END button on the second ring.

Don't overthink it.

Do it all in one sitting. It's one page, for crying out loud. It's your life; you are your own research. Don't waste days looking up dates and calling your old companies and friends to document details. While you're investigating, others are getting hired.

Don't start with your "career objective."

This says, "Hi, I'm an amateur." Unless you are a recent college grad, I don't care what you want; I care about what my company needs done. We'll talk about what *you* want at your second interview, when I'm trying to make you happy. Remember, what I really want is to screen you out. Don't make it easier for me.

A reverse chronology is the proper format.

Tell me who you work for now, in what capacity, and what your duties and functions are. Do this for the most recent decade. If you're old enough to have previous decades, you may summarize them, since no one really cares but you, and even you can't remember the "you" of your early résumé.

Bragging rights: your achievements and accomplishments.

This is critical. Tell me, in a *quantitative way*, about your performance in each job. Show me how you will make me money or save me money. I'm looking at the résumé of a guy I recently placed. Here's one of his entries:

WIREFORCE Inc. (Second largest manufacturer of wire-molded products in the U.S.)
Director of Quality Assurance (2002–present)
Complete budgetary responsibility of a 15 million dollar Quality unit comprised of 127 people. This includes 45 engineers and 12 research scientists.
- Reduced failure rate 89 percent in first year
- Eliminated 2nd shift of inspection, saving 12 million dollars
- Won the auto industry's coveted QAA award
- Designed team innovations that reduced lead time by 122 percent

This guy is a pro. That's why I placed him and earned a commission of 43K. He doesn't spell out the details or worry about making sure you know exactly when all this happened. He doesn't stress over whether he's taking too much credit for things that obviously involved other people. He understood his résumé as an advertisement. You want more info? You want to know how he did it? Interview him!

Depending on your area of expertise, it may be perfectly acceptable to include the following in your "bragging rights":

- Patents
- Awards
- Education (If really impressive and recent. If you were a 4.0 at a state school and you're 40, let it go.)
- Rate of promotion
- Publications
- Design innovations
- Major clients sold or serviced (If it's a household name, use it. We all love branding.)

Affiliations and/or civic interests.

If you're committed to a career, you can demonstrate that by showing me associations and/or extra training and certification. It shows consistency of purpose. And if in your busy life you have found the time for charitable work or you are active in some civic way that shows you care about the world around you, go ahead and include it—briefly! As a small and petty person, I do not like to hire morally superior people. I admire you; I just don't see what we have in common.

Family and personal situation.

I know your family is the most important thing in the world to you. Mine is to me. It's a given. Givens don't get space on a one-page résumé. Don't tell me you have two "healthy beautiful daughters named Hazel and Greta and that you married your high school sweetheart." This is a résumé, not your acceptance speech for a lifetime achievement award. You could also be creating a negative. Maybe the job has travel, and they're going to assume you won't be available. Maybe the hiring authority's kids are the bane of his existence or she just got divorced. Wait until you read the situation in an interview, and then by all means, if needed, wax poetic about the wonders of family.

When all else fails, tell the truth.

Just because I said earlier your résumé is an advertisement, that is not a license to steal. It's been estimated that as much as 40 percent of what is on a résumé is exaggerated or is an outright untruth: you leave out short stays that didn't work out and merge your dates of employment to show continuity that inconveniently didn't take place; you figure you went to college for three years and did a lot of course work, so why not say you have a degree? You didn't head up the project, but you know your boss is no longer there, and who's to say now that it's so long ago, and hell, you *could* have headed up the project—you worked so damn hard on it . . .

Don't do it! If you lie in the résumé and are caught, nothing will save you. They will not hire you, or if they do and then find out you lied, they will fire you. And I will tell them to do so, since a) that means you lied to me, and b) my interest is in the next deal with this client, and I'm not sullying my reputation to save you.

Here's the saving grace about truth on résumés. Companies hire people who have been fired, people who flunk drug tests, and people who lost major accounts—but only if you come clean *before the fact*. Companies love to forgive; they do not tolerate being played for fools. Don't take the risk; it's just not worth it.

Now don't procrastinate. Go write your résumé before you read the next section. And don't freak out about how the damn thing looks. Don't use logos—the nipple rings of résumés—use a basic Roman font, use white or ivory colored paper, don't use anything smaller than 10-point type, and remember that less is more. Clutter is bad; white space is good. That's all you need to know. Now sit yourself down and write. It's your life. It should flow. It's the ultimate "me" time. Enjoy it. When you're done, you should be reading it and feeling, "I would *totally* hire me!"

If Harper asks me about his chapter on writing résumés, I am going to tell him it was inspiring and I cranked out a draft in twenty minutes. But by nature I buck the system, so I checked if my gym clothes passed the smell test and headed for my work-out. But I was thinking of my résumé the entire fifteen-minute drive down the Merritt Parkway.

I had "bragging rights," as Harper calls them. I have a degree in marketing from a decent school, and while I'm not a programmer, I can fake the tech talk so well most CIOs try to recruit me. I'm attractive—not crazy, jaw-dropping attractive; I'm a child short of being a MILF—and in the prime of my career. Writing the résumé should be simple, given Harper's notes. So why did I have to do a spin class in order to buck up the courage? Was it because I not only had no husband or children to brag about, but because like a startup company's website, that part of my résumé would read "currently under construction"?

Spin classes are all about the instructor and the music. Today I got Eva, a Nazi born long after her time, who kept telling me to keep my butt down, thereby drawing attention to my butt, and who is fond of country and western tunes for the long climbs. I decided as I walked out that spin was not going to make the cut on my résumé's "personal interests" section.

On my way to the locker I saw Cute Guy walking toward me. This was entirely the wrong angle to look at *his* butt, but these are life's little burdens, and I settled for his face, which was, I now noticed, really amazing. Soft brown eyes; sharp, almost jutting jaw; and silly high cheekbones. But is he scowling at me? I smiled and said "Hi," and he dismissively rolled his eyes, said, "Right," and walked by me.

Whatever, buddy. Nice to know my beacon for psychos stays lit like the Olympic torch.

The workout didn't provide the attitude adjustment needed to revamp my résumé. I thought about Harper predicting that video résumés would soon be the accepted format and that the capabilities already exist. I did a Google search and found ProHire-View. The mechanics were simple. For a nominal yearly fee, you could record a video in lieu of the written résumé and attach it to a written profile. They would pretty it up and format it into a professional looking product that they would then send out for you. All you had to do was send them the URLs and job postings. If you had Windows Media and a webcam, you could record and attach within their site.

I decided that I had to try to differentiate myself through the coolest new technique, and it would help me "rough draft" some thoughts in my head. I got out my credit card, joined up, and read through the short tutorial. Hell, you sit in front of the screen and click RECORD—I think I can handle it.

I showered, did my hair and make-up, and dressed for cyber success. Seventy-five minutes and four auditioned outfits later, I sat down in front of my webcam, cleared my throat, and double-clicked on RECORD.

"Good morning."

I hit the STOP and REPLAY buttons. How the hell did I know what time they would be watching this, whoever they are?

"Hi, I'm Casey Matthews. I've attached my résumé in text format, but I wanted you to know something more about me through the wonders of video. As you can see, I've spent my eleven-year career in software sales, mostly in the financial services and supply chain space. In college I took several psychological tests, purely for vocational reasons, and I tested very high for sales. They turned out to be right: I was SAP's top North-eastern rep by the time I was twenty-seven. I took a New York City territory from zero to eight million dollars in fifteen months, opening accounts like Bank of America and Goldman Sachs. My ambition, after more sales seasoning and more years of record-setting production, would be sales management, and eventually marketing or strategy management. I look forward to speaking with you soon. My contact info is attached."

I hit STOP. What a bunch of crap! It's what they want to hear, and as I replayed it, I decided it wasn't half bad. That made me more upset. I hit RECORD again.

"Casey Matthews here, opting for honesty. I need a job. You have posted an opening. And there you have it. I quit my last job. I was doing well. I could have stayed. You don't believe me? I don't blame you. Who does that? At the time, I felt my life lacked meaning and that I was at a crossroads. Now my life lacks meaning *and* income, and I remain at the crossroads. But let's cut to the chase. Look at my résumé. I can sell. Call me in the next ninety minutes and I'll knock ten percent off my salary."

I hit STOP, played it back, and hit ERASE. I sat back on my couch and remembered going to the primary school where my sister teaches for Career Day. My niece Sheila was going to talk about her parents' jobs. Todd is an ophthalmologist. Sheila stood in front of the class and said, "My mommy helps little kids become smarter, and Daddy makes sure people can see the things they need to see." My heart didn't break, but there was a hairline fracture.

I sat up and hit RECORD.

"My name is Casey, and I'm a little lost. I'm a complete control freak, and yet I have never really had control. I truly believe love conquers all, and yet I can never summon the courage to fight for it. I sell because I want people, usually men, to like me, and then I resent them when I pull it off. I want to be smarter, but instead of reading I watch movies. I want to be patient and kinder, but everyone bores me except Harper, and the longer I am unemployed even he is wearing thin. I am so scared and so furious at myself for being weak enough to be scared. Thanks for your time."

I hit ERASE, sat at my desk, and tried to decide if crying would help. And then I heard the chirp of a text message.

I have an interview for you! Say goodbye and thanks to your host at the pity party and meet me at the Darien Country Club at 4 P.M. Dress like a golfer.

Harper, I never doubted you! Suddenly, almost magically, I was sick of being sick of myself. I sat down and wrote my résumé in twenty-five minutes. Now, how do you dress like a golfer?

CHAPTER SIX

NETWORKING, JOB BOARDS, AND DATING ONLINE

Harper read through my résumé in seven seconds, nodded, folded it in half, and stuffed it in his golf bag. I glared at him.

"What? I don't need your résumé. The rest of the world does."

"Then why did you make me crazy over it?"

"Because you need it to bring to interviews and attach to postings, and frankly, it kept you from bugging me. I have a job to do and a book to write. The life of an artist is exhausting."

He took out a micro recorder. He didn't look exhausted. I thought we were having lunch, but instead I had a pile of balls and some women's rental clubs. Harper had his director's chair, a glass of iced tea, and an umbrella to shade himself. For the fifth straight time, I swung back with the driver and hit the green rubber mat five inches behind the ball. I looked at Harper furiously, but he held his finger over his lips. He turned the recorder on and said, "Finding Your Own Job—High Touch and High Tech."

He looked at me and pressed PAUSE.

"What? I'll have my secretary transcribe it. Don't be so judgmental. Turn your left shoulder behind the ball, but don't lift your head."

I swung at the ball and this time hit it sideways into the wooden wall that bordered my station, and it bounced back at me. I shrieked and jumped out of the way. Harper sensed his imminent danger, took a club out of my bag, and motioned for me to move aside.

He set himself, waggled, and then made a long, languid pass at the ball. It was as if he wasn't trying to hit the ball; he just let the shot happen. The ball rocketed off the ground and went so high into the sky and so deep down the range that it went past all the markers. Harper put the club back in the bag without even waiting to see where the ball dropped.

"Look, Bagger Vance, what about the interview you said you had for me?"

"We're not here just to talk about your interview. I am going to teach you how you can get even more interviews without me by utilizing your network. People find their own jobs 86 percent of the time. Headhunters, Internet job sites, and career boards kill themselves for a small portion of the pie that would be smaller if people knew what they were doing. So I'm going to tell you and record it, so I get a chapter out of it. That's called a win/win."

"But there is an interview, right?"

"I have an interview for you. We just need to pick a day that matches everyone's schedule."

"But why golf? It can't be that much fun for you to see me make a fool of myself."

"It's not only not fun for me, it's excruciating. But necessary."

Harper looked behind me and smiled the smug smile of someone whose plan was being executed without flaw. An older man, immaculately dressed, was walking to the practice bunkers with a sand wedge and a small bucket of balls. Harper waved to him, and the man came over to us. They exchanged the obligatory male trash talking, and then Harper introduced me.

"This is Casey Matthews. Casey, Wallace Avery."

"So you're Casey? Harper didn't say you played golf."

"Well, it's been a while. Trying to get back into it."

"My advice would be not to bother. But then, you know what? Once in a great while, one of the little white suckers actually goes where you aimed it, and it's all worthwhile. Nice meeting you, Casey."

And he walked away. Nice guy. Had a charm about him, a breezy sort of confidence. He was downright sexy, and he had to be close to seventy. I have been alone way, way too long.

"Who is he, Harper?"

"He is the exec VP and a major stockholder in the software company you're interviewing with. InterAnnex Software."

"That's why we're here? You knew he'd be here this time of day?"

"He's late. I thought he'd be here two buckets ago. Let's go eat."

I used to think golfers sat in the grill rooms at their clubs in order to recount shots that everyone around the table already saw and to drink rather than go home to their families.

I still think so.

But as Harper and I had lunch and he positioned his micro recorder on the table, I understood what Harper was after by bringing me here. I recognized three of my old customers, presidents of banks I had sold enterprise-wide software to; two IT directors who had run seminars I had attended; and a couple of competitors of my old company. All in the same room, in good moods. Harper lured all of them over and introduced me. He never said I was looking for a job; he never even said what business I was in. None of them recognized me, even the customers I had met several times and relieved of millions of their company's dollars. When Harper found his opening and made it clear I was a client, "a former superstar at SAP," they gave me business cards and asked for my number.

I had done a month's worth of networking, and all I had to do was sit there and occasionally say things like, "So, who won all the skins and greenies and sandies?" My only gaffe occurred when my cell phone went off at the table. The golf course and grill room were the last refuge from otherwise constant connectivity. I looked down quickly at the number. Peter Bonetti again! How the hell did he get my cell phone? This geek has crossed over from tenacity to harassment. I powered down my cell as Harper cleared his throat and began his chapter.

"So what's the first lesson of finding your own job, Casey?"

"Uh, get a job as a cart girl?"

"Gee, I'm sorry, I thought you were unemployed and needed help. When is open mike night?"

"Okay, Harper, the first lesson, obviously, is you need to leverage your contacts before you send out résumés to people who know nothing about you."

Harper shook his head and leaned in. He really was passionate about this stuff, even after all these years. Was he this passionate at home, with his wife and daughter? He clicked the power button on the micro recorder without losing eye contact.

HARPER'S RULES
Finding Your Own Job—High Touch and High Tech.

The first lesson in finding your own job is understanding that high touch comes before high tech.

Tactic 1: Before you turn to the Internet postings or the Sunday classifieds, you put your personal supply chain on notice.

Everyone has a personal supply chain. We think of supply chains as things companies have when they want to schedule, distribute, track, and ship product. Walmart uses a vendor supply chain to make product and get it in the stores.

And that's true of every working professional on the planet. You have a supply chain of vendors who have a vested interest in your welfare. If you're like most professionals, you have a supply chain already in place. A travel agent? Personal trainer? Jeweler? Real estate agent? An accountant? A lawyer? A psychologist or therapist? Housekeeper? How about all of your doctors? Your dentist, your vet? The guy who set up your high-def TV?

Every one of these people should be alerted to your need for a job or a future relationship. Any one of these people could refer you to someone who knows someone who might be 'the someone' who could hire you or fix you up.

"Sorry to interrupt, Harper; I know you're making this up as you go along. But how does telling my housekeeper or the guy at Jiffy Lube help me get a job as a senior sales rep, to say nothing of how they would know the kind of person who is right for me to date?"

Harper sat back stiffly. "You, Casey Matthews, are a snob." He leaned in toward the recorder again.

Six degrees of separation doesn't discriminate. It knows no boundaries. It has no attitude. You don't know who people know. You think they don't have a sense of judgment because they have low incomes? You think their powers of observation are limited by their station in life?

"Okay, enough. I feel terrible about myself. I will contact my personal supply chain and let them know what my needs are. But it's hard."

"Sure, because you're proud. How's that working out for you? Let that go and you'll be surprised how much more help you'll get from people and how much more they'll like you."

I thought of all the nights since the divorce, and more nights since I have been unemployed, when the phone hasn't made a sound. I have made it a lifelong habit to convince those around me I have no needs; they all assume I'm okay. I instantly made a pact with myself to come clean with everyone in my personal supply chain as Harper continued.

"People want to help, but the power of word of mouth has to come from you. You have to be willing to ask the two questions that have made me wealthy: Can I ask you for some help? Who do you know?

Tactic 2: Call your professional references. Let them know that you are active in the job market and ask them if you can count on them for a recommendation.

Do this for *all* of your old jobs. These people could hire you back or recommend you for a position they know about.

It's wise to include colleagues as business references. Do you know why? Because they receive recruiting calls from headhunters like me! Seventy percent of the time they hear the headhunter out and even send a résumé out of sheer curiosity. But they don't take a new job; they flirt. They may even interview, but they turn down the eventual offer. They are the bane of any good headhunter's existence, but they are useful to you. If they have turned down an offer, they feel guilty and want to help the headhunter out. If they know you are looking or have your résumé in their email, you may get a position on the rebound.

Tactic 3: You need to be working with two headhunters that specialize in your niche, market space, or industry vertical.

Why two? Because no one headhunter has access to all the opportunities. But limit it to only two reputable firms.

Never shotgun your résumé to every headhunter posting you see online. Headhunters, especially those working at the contingency level—they only get a fee when the placement is made and the candidate has begun work—all have the same jobs. You'll dilute your own efforts and become persona non grata.

"So, Harper, you're saying I need to be working with another headhunter besides you?"

Harper clicked off the recorder and glared at me again.

"You're riding Secretariat, love. You don't need to get on the merry-go-round."

He reached over to click the recorder back on, but I had a question, so I placed my hand over his, and there was a weird moment where we both realized we were touching each other.

"Harper, I know you because you came after me a long time ago. But what about the people who are going to read your book who don't know who the connected headhunters are?"

He pressed the RECORD button.

Insider tip to find the best headhunters:

Call the VP of human resources at any of the companies that compete with your last place of employment. The amateur move is to ask them who they would recommend you work with as a search firm; headhunters call HR all the time. But the insider move is to ask them which headhunters they really hate. Who are the ones that try to circumvent them and go straight to the line managers? Who are the ones that have stolen their best people? The headhunters that the human resources people hate the most are the ones you want working for you.

"Okay, you ready? High touch before high tech, tactic four: the big one—the secret of how headhunters get jobs! Learn this skill and you'll never need me or Internet job postings or classified ads again!"

He looked so serious that I had to consider if Harper no longer being a necessary part of my life was something I wanted or not. Without me in job crisis, would he care enough to stay in touch? Before I could decide, Harper pulled out his vibrating Blackberry. He clicked, read for a few seconds, and then shook his head slowly. I have been in sales long enough to know he had just lost a deal.

"This clown is a director of marketing in Redwood City, making 160K. I got him an offer for 240K, but the commute is an hour longer. He's turning it down."

"Quality-of-life issue, right?" I offered.

"Nah, it's an excuse. He's scared." Harper signed the check and stood up. "I gotta go deal with this. You know, Casey, that's another way relationships and jobs are the same: If you love someone, you don't tell him he lives too far away so you can't see him anymore. You drive faster."

"Hold it, Harper. You can't make me keep my cell off while yours was on, promise an interview about which I still know nothing, tell me you're about to share the secret of finding a job, and then ditch me. What if you die on the Merritt Parkway on the way to your office? I won't get my interview, the secret will die with you, and I could be unemployed forever!"

"And . . . there'd be the tragedy of my demise."

"Oh, right. That too. Give me the PowerPoint version right now."

Harper sighed and sat down.

"Let's role-play it. You are the senior VP of sales and marketing at a major software company. Your goal is simple: drive revenue. You are sitting at your desk. The phone rings, and here I come: 'Casey, my name is Harper Scott. Have you heard of me? I'm a headhunter who focuses on your industry; I've built sales teams for your competitors: people like Jake Malcom at Intellivision and Bob Peters at Odeon Systems. I'm reaching out because I've recruited a killer, one of SAP's big stars: a woman personally responsible for scoring accounts like Amex and Deutsche Bank, sales of over 12 million dollars in two years. She is putting out feelers to make a move, and I wanted you to have a shot at talking to her. How did I do in getting your attention?'"

It was strange to realize that Harper had just pitched me to me—even stranger to realize I was impressed.

"That's what you do, Harper? That's how you get your work? I guess I thought it was more glamorous."

"Do I make smart calls to my network first? Sure. But I still do cold canvassing because it generates new work, keeps my skills sharp, and exposes new niches and trends in the marketplace. Basics, baby. For most headhunters, fifty calls each morning to start the day. It's called 'prime calling hours with an MPC.'"

"MPC?"

"That's you, kiddo. Most Placeable Candidate."

Tactic 4: How headhunters get their search assignments, and how you can cut out the middle man and do it for yourself.

Headhunters' Most Placeable Candidates are:

1. Most talented (verified by quantifiable track record)
2. Most available and motivated to take a job
3. Most skilled in presenting themselves physically (It's a shallow world; what can I say?)
4. Most flexible in the way of location and commute
5. Most reasonable in their compensation parameters

Once they have their list, they gather a list of companies who are most likely, based on your work history, to be interested in your background, and they pitch you by voice mail, live connects, and email, fifty times a day.

And that is Tactic Four. No headhunter should be more effective at doing this for you than you! A headhunter works with many different MPCs and many different search assignments at any one time; you only get a fraction of their attention and time. You just have to have the guts to make the call!

To make your own MPC call, follow these steps:

1. Generate a list of companies (competitors) that should have an interest in your background, based on your last five years of work history. You can use Internet tools as generic as Google or as specific as Hoovers, Broadlook, or Zoom Info.
2. Find the line manager you would report to. See if her profile or direct number is on the website before making the call.
3. As a backup, you can go to the human resources department . . . but only as a backup.
4. You will probably get a voice mail. You must leave a compelling message that is thirty seconds, tops! The goal is a call back, not applause.
5. Present your background in a highlight-film format. Three bullet points of accomplishments and achievements. Let them know you are reaching out to a few players you respect and would like to talk to them about their needs.
6. Keep the enthusiasm high and the vibe positive. You are not making this call out of need; you are exploring options!
7. When they call back, close on an interview. "When can we talk about this live?"
8. Don't discuss salary or anything of personal convenience on a phone interview or via email. An MPC's goal is to get an interview.

"That's it, Casey. A good MPC gets three interviews for every fifty calls made by an experienced headhunter. Your ratio should be better because no one has as much knowledge about you as you do, and no one has more at stake."

"But it seems so simple, Harper. Why wouldn't everyone do that for themselves before they called you?"

"Because they're afraid. The same reason we don't tell someone we love that we love them, even though we might ache to do so. What if they reject us?"

I had to look away. Harper clicked off his recorder and stood up. This writing session was over.

"Well, I'm not afraid. I'm a salesperson. I can make those calls."

"I know," Harper said, "and you should. Gotta go."

"What about the interview?"

"A little faith, please."

Harper moved past me, touched my shoulder briefly but not absently, and squeezed for a second.

Suddenly I felt another hand pat my shoulder. Is there a sign on my back that says, PAT HERE, I'M LONELY?

"So," Wallace Avery began, "it seems Harper has left us to our own devices. Sorry, did I startle you?"

"No, I'm sorry, just preoccupied. Backswing, downswing, straight left arm . . ."

He smiled. "Well, we need to schedule our meeting. How's ten on Friday? I'm in Stamford on Fridays, so I can save you the drive in to Manhattan. The Archer Building across from the Marriott."

"I look forward to it. Look at us, doing Harper's job for him."

"Well," Wallace shrugged, "I'm sure it's awkward for him."

I must have looked confused.

"You know, don't you?" he said.

"I'm not sure what you're referring to."

"We passed a corporate edict a year ago: no more headhunting fees. If we end up hiring you, Harper is not charging us."

Wallace could see he had made me uncomfortable but was not to be deterred by my burst of pride.

"He told me he's placed you twice, young lady, and I have paid him a small fortune over the years, so you and I have earned this, and we are going to meet Friday. Besides, we may hate you. Friday. Okay?"

"I'll be there."

"First test. Can you be trusted with a secret? I just talked out of school, and now you need to cover for me with Harper."

Halfway home, I decided I had to breach the confidentiality with Wallace and talk to Harper. Should I thank him? Should I rip into him and tell him I do not need charity and that if he was going to change the nature of our business relationship he should have included me in the decision? Harper's fee for someone on my level was around 40K! But what if he told Wallace Avery that I knew? It not only would cost me the job I had not yet interviewed for; how would I feel when Avery asked me why I broke his trust?

I once asked Harper if he could keep a secret because I wanted to tell him some juicy gossip I had heard about a major competitor's product. "No," he said solemnly, "I can't keep a secret. If you tell me I will tell everyone I know. Then I'll start cold calling."

I made a decision to respect Avery's wishes and keep Harper's pro bono work to myself.

I was pulling into my driveway, trying to figure out why this lovely gesture on Harper's part had somehow made me resentful of him, when my cell buzzed, and I saw the name and number of Peter Bonetti. I will eat this clown alive.

"Peter Bonetti, as I live and breathe." There was a pause. "Well?"

"Okay, give me a minute. I'm so used to your voice mail recording, I never considered you might actually pick up."

I sat back in my car seat in my driveway. This was going to be so much fun.

"Well, that's a rookie move, Peter. You are supposed to be prepared for a live connect every time you reach out to someone like me."

"You haven't made it easy. Didn't anyone ever teach you the basic courtesy of returning someone's call?"

Okay, this kid is going to die, and then I'm going after his family. "Are you joking? How many times have you called me? Ten, fifteen?"

"Six on your regular phone and three on your cell. Not that I'm tracking it."

"God, you really are a rookie, aren't you? How long have you been doing this?"

"You mean calling women I don't know and trying to get them to give me a few minutes before they reject me?"

"Exactly. How long?"

"About six months, I guess. I used to think I was pretty good at this. But I've been out of it for so long, guess I don't have my game back yet."

I knew guys like this. They get out of sales because they burn out, and then when they try to get back in, they've lost their nerve.

"Okay, rookie. I'm going to cut you a break and let you make your pitch. It's not going to work, but I'll let you practice. Go."

"I don't think so. Enough is enough. Thanks for taking my call. You really need to learn some manners."

"Give me your manager's name, Bonetti!"

"What? What are you talking about?"

"I want your manager's name."

"I don't have a manager. My boss is the owner, and you know him. I've seen you talk to him."

"Okay, stop trying to confuse me. Who is this owner?"

"Just make sure when you talk to him you admit that I have caught you staring at my ass. That you flirt with me. That you told Amanda at the front desk that I was hot, which is why I looked you up in the member's database and got your cell phone. That is against gym rules, so go ahead and get me fired. At least I won't have to see you anymore."

Oh my God! Peter Bonetti is Cute Guy! No wonder he gave me the stinkeye the last couple of times I saw him. I started to laugh. I wanted to tell him I had never listened to any of his messages, but when I tried, nothing came out but a snorting sound, and then I lost it and was laughing so hard I was crying. I couldn't remember the last time I had laughed so hard. Finally I calmed down enough to explain. At first I could tell he didn't believe me, but then he surrendered, and he started to laugh—a deep, savory laugh that I could tell he gave up easily under normal circumstances. To me it was a precious, vulnerable piece of me I dispensed with stinginess. I make men laugh; they don't make me laugh.

"I'm sorry, Peter. Really, I am. You know if you wore the polo shirt with the name tag that all the other gym employees wear instead of the tank tops you walk around in, I'd have known your name."

"I'm a personal trainer; those tank tops get me business."

"Right," I laughed.

"Can I make my pitch now?"

"Sure."

"I work at the gym as a personal trainer. I don't have a lot of money, although my client base is growing. I am thirty-two years old, and I was living with a girl for five years who pretty much broke my heart about six months ago. I'm really afraid of going through all that again but decided it was time to take a risk. You seemed, I don't know . . ."

"This is where you say, 'really, really hot.'"

"That too, sure, but you seemed like . . . you'd been there. Like you were trying to act okay."

"I am okay," I managed, finally.

"Okay. So I wanted to see if you wanted to do something in the area of a date of some sort."

"That's your pitch?"

"There it is."

"It's pretty weak, Peter. I have had classical sales training, and you are breaking all the rules. You are supposed to only present your best qualities, not your weaknesses, and then of course you didn't close me on a specific time. The correct method would be to ask an open ended question like, 'How's Saturday?'"

"Saturday's great. What time?"

Oh no, I'm feeling that flutter thing in my chest. I promised myself to never feel that again.

"I don't know, Peter, I just don't know if I can. I'm sorry."

"I understand."

"Oh for God's sake, that's an objection! You're supposed to overcome it. All right! Seven o'clock on Saturday. Hang up the phone now, Peter. A good salesman gets the order and gets off the phone."

An interview on Friday and a date on Saturday . . . Could things be starting to actually go my way? Dial down the hope, I told myself. It's the hope that gets you.

CHAPTER SEVEN

PREPPING FOR INTERVIEWS AND DATES

The next day I went running at Hubbard Park. I hate running outside, but I have a quandary: I need to lose two to five pounds in the three days before my interview and date, but the person I am dating works at the gym and would see me trying to overcompensate.

Just when I was trying to decide whether to do the mile loop again or head back home, a car pulled up and a young kid rolled down the window. Here we go. Boys and their turbo-testosterone. What can you do?

"Excuse me, ma'am," he said politely, "do you know where Webster's Bakery is?"

"Are you crazy? You stop me while I'm running and not only don't give me a 'hey, baby,' but when you saw me from behind, you thought, 'there's someone who knows where a bakery is?'"

"Sorry, ma'am."

He drove off and I felt the urge to memorize the license plate, but I didn't know whom I would report them to. Then I heard the laughter. I turned to square off with my next victim, and there was Harper on a park bench by the jogging trail.

He was wearing a houndstooth sport coat and a cashmere sweater over an oxford shirt, and had a Burberry trench coat folded in his lap. The cordovan loafers were so polished they looked like they had just been taken out of their shoebox for the first time.

"Hey, baby. How was that?"

"Tread lightly, funny man. What are you doing here, Harper?"

"You have an interview. It's my job to prep you for that interview, and everything I tell you will also apply to the date you told me you have on Saturday."

"Another book chapter."

"You're so cynical. We need to get you a job so you can go back to just being disgruntled."

"But how did you know I'd be here? I haven't run outside in months!"

"I didn't know. I was taking a chance you'd be home and was on your street when you ran by. Why aren't you at your gym—oh, never mind. Your date is with someone you met there, and you can't risk looking overanxious."

"Does your wife find your deductive powers as annoying as I do?"

He stood up. "Do you want to walk? I need to give you my chapter and then get to work."

It wasn't really a question; Harper started walking. I reminded him that I had always done well on interviews.

"That's nonsense," Harper said. "I track my ratios. Without a headhunter's professional prep, even excellent candidates get offers only forty percent of the time. With the prep, it's seventy percent. And how about dating; how are your ratios there?"

"I never tracked my dating ratios, Harper, seeing as how I'm not a psycho."

"You should. It's a numbers game. Why waste your time? Can I begin, or do you need to sit at the next bench and catch your breath?"

"No need to be snippy."

HARPER'S RULES
Prepping for Interviews and First Dates

Rule #1: Know your objective: to be asked back for a second interview or another date.

You may turn down that invitation, but you can't go into the interview/date with any thought other than getting them to want you. Sure, sometimes it's just a courtesy interview or a blind date and you find yourself woefully mismatched. In that case, just stand up, tell them you value their time as well as your own, but know instinctively this won't work. Thank them for their time and move on. But this scenario is rare.

Most of the time the first interview/date protocol makes it impossible to determine your interest level. Everyone is on their best behavior. As an unemployed/single person, you have a vested interest in giving them the benefit of the doubt. If your mindset is that you have one objective only—to get another meeting—you will be more aware of the most important dynamic in first interviews and dates: it's all about them!

Rule #2: It's all about them.

Meeting One is about their needs and desires. Your goal is to show them you are truly present and really listening while they are talking. On a first meeting, imagine you're their ghostwriter, helping them write their memoirs. We all love to talk about ourselves. If you make it your business to leave that date or that interview knowing 1) that you have actively asked them about their lives; and 2) that you have left them wanting to know more about your life, you will get asked if you are available for another meeting, and that is the only way of knowing the first interview or date was a success.

Rule #3: Never go on an interview or a date without having done your homework.
The more you know going into the meeting, the more power you have; and the more power you have, the more you control the outcome. We live in a search-engine world, and yet the majority of the people who walk into interviews have done zero research about the company or the person they are meeting. They walk into an office with a résumé, hand it over, and then sit back and allow themselves to be interrogated. This is all wrong. I instruct all my candidates to control the interview by showing, through a series of questions and statements, that they are knowledgeable, curious to learn more, and razor-sharp. These are all attractive traits, and we want to be with or work with people we find attractive.

So, *never* go on an interview without knowing:
- Company history
- Company products or service (and their value proposition in the market)
- Who the customers and/or end users are
- Size of company and number of employees
- Whether they are publicly or privately traded and if public, what the current stock value is
- Work history of the person(s) you are meeting
- The culture of the firm
- An understanding of and empathy for the short-term problems they are facing

And if you can, you need shock-and-awe information! Something they will be amazed you found out. Something that says "This one is different."

Now, you don't roll all this out at once; it's not a book report. You work it in. You let it develop organically.

Harper could read the look on my face. I'm a note person. Not having my Blackberry made me feel uncomfortable, but I couldn't bring myself to carry it in a pocket and have it bang against my thigh when I was only 500 yards from my house. If I really was so out of shape that I needed it to call 9-1-1 because I couldn't make it 500 yards back, I felt like I deserved to die.

Harper assured me that he was giving me the synopsis and that in the folder all of this was documented in a longer form.

I told him I already read the website of InterAnnex, the company he had set me up with, and had read the bio on their site of Wallace Avery. He shrugged. Okay, I wasn't looking for a shrug; I wanted approval. God, when will I stop needing approval? My therapist tells me it's key for my personal growth. But I know if I ever pull it off, I'll call her to tell her so she'll be proud of me.

"Let's take InterAnnex as a case study," he said. "I have taken the liberty of doing your homework for you, since I am using your interview in my book and paying you not one dime of future royalties. Now, InterAnnex is a software company in the social networking market vertical. When you go in to meet Wallace, unlike your competition, you will be able to tell him that you know they began in 2002, with only four employees as an instant messaging company, with a simple product. Then they built the Six Degrees Platform, mindful that Facebook was growing by leaps and bounds, and basically became a startup for a second time. In 2006 they were backed by Adobe Ventures to the tune of 50 million dollars. They are now thirty-one employees, mostly technicians, but with a 40 million dollar pipeline of referenceable customers.

"They have no sales force. That's where you come in. *Fortune* magazine calls social networking the first original form of marketing in a generation, and *The Wall Street Journal* says social networking is in its embryonic stages and will compete with nano-technology for the most important innovation of the twenty-first century. My search is for their first VP of sales."

I knew what Harper was doing, but I was getting excited anyway. I just wanted to be in my interview already. "What do you know about Wallace that isn't on the website?"

"You already know he's a golfer. But that's too easy. Wallace put his career on hold in early 1991, even though he was already a very successful marketing guy in the logistics space. You know why? Because his dad was in the military and fought in the Pacific. Two Purple Hearts. During Vietnam, Wallace didn't protest, he served. But no action. Stayed in the reserves after that, and when they needed logistics expertise in Kuwait and Iraq, Wallace asked for a leave of absence and off he went. He was fifty-two years old. He told me it wasn't a sense of duty as much as he felt he was still owed some action, so when he asks you why you want to start your sales career in a new product space you know nothing about . . ."

"I tell him sales still owes me some action. He'll know it came from you, Harper."

"We've never discussed it. I was holding it back for a special occasion. Besides, even if he did know it was from me, use it anyway. By the way, his daughter Sara did an internship for the same congressman you did, so even if you spent that summer sneaking out to get high in the Smithsonian restrooms, you might want to recall it fondly for Wallace."

We had reached my house, and I saw that Harper's Range Rover was parked two houses down from my driveway. Harper checked his watch and handed me the folder.

"Do you make house calls for everyone, Harper?"

"How well have you been listening? What have I left out?"

"Shock and awe; something that says I'm different. Well? Don't hold out on me now; I've postponed my shower and post–runner's high nap for you. Give."

"Cisco is going to buy them. Could be as much as 2 billion. As soon as they prove they have a sales model that works. Wallace is already rich; he is about to get silly rich."

"So if I get in now, will I get a piece of that?"

Harper took his index finger and shook it at me like we had just played hide and seek and he found me in the first place he looked.

"There is nothing hotter than an opportunistic, beautiful, sweaty, gross woman. Would I be sending you there if you couldn't get a piece of that?"

Harper pointed his keys at the Rover; lights went off and the latches opened on all four doors.

"Casey, two more things: One, everything we just went through should be applied to Peter Bonetti before this weekend; and two, start asking yourself how you will answer the question Wallace asks everyone: 'If you had this job, who would you sell to first?'"

"Wait. How would I know who to sell to first?"

"You do know. Trust yourself."

Trust myself. That's really good advice, and I plan on doing that one of these days.

As soon as I got back from the interview, I emailed Harper:

Harper,

I just got back from my interview with InterAnnex and Wallace Avery, and I thought these notes might help you in the unlikely event you ever get serious about your book. Don't bother to thank me. Splitting your publisher's advance will do.

Let me say, first of all: *I. Nailed. It.*

Second, I do not need your advice in choosing the appropriate look or clothes for an interview. I'm not saying you shouldn't advise others in your book; I'm saying you don't need to advise *me* in those areas, since I dress for every sales call I ever go on and because you are not a woman. When I awoke to your one-word text message, "Pants," I realized you have been married too long.

Did I mention? *I. Nailed. It.*

Let me walk you through some tips for your readers. No charge, by the way.

HARPER'S RULES
Addendum on Interviewing, written for Harper Scott by Casey Matthews

Rule #1: Dress for every interview.

Dress conservatively. Don't overdo jewelry or make-up or perfume or cologne, and wear formal business attire even if you know it's a casual work environment.

Rule #2: Get there early, but not "psycho" early.

Don't make the interviewer think you have nothing else to do all day! And when you arrive, make friends with the receptionist. Sometime you may need him or her to put your call through to your potential new boss.

Rule #3: Travel light.

Take your coat off and carry a light briefcase or valise. You don't want to ruin your cool by dragging your gear down hallways.

Rule #4: Be more awake than the rest of the humans that day.

If the consciousness level in the office is a 5 out of 10, you need to be a 7. (A 9 or 10 is over the top, and you'll wear out your welcome.) "If you don't have an enthusiasm that is contagious, whatever you do have is also contagious" is the first and best rule of communication.

Rule #5: Shake hands firmly but don't grit your teeth and arm wrestle.

Rule #6: No obvious or phony compliments.

And no matter how nice the building or office, say nothing. You expect him to have a nice office, and you want him hoping he's living up to your expectations.

Rule #7: No negatives.

Never bad-mouth a previous employer. It doesn't matter how unfair the situation was or how screwed over you were, you simply say it didn't work out. They will see you as someone who will be accountable.

Rule #8. Have fun!

It's not life or death. It's the one time you can brag legitimately!

You know what Harper? Now that I think about it, you should thank me.

I hit SEND and fell back into my post-interview afterglow. Why does everyone tout the grace of losers or the character building of being humbled? Winning works! Why do they try to tell us otherwise? I hit a home run on my interview. I still got it, big time; no one can keep me from savoring the moment.

Except Harper. He called immediately after reading my email. When someone changes the mode of communication, you know you got to them.

"Hi, Harper. I hope you don't mind that my portion of your book is actually written down."

"How did you handle the money discussion, Casey?"

There was an edge in his voice.

"What do you mean?"

"Did Wallace ask you how much money you wanted?"

"Yes. I told him I wanted a base of 200K and commission potential to double that. What? Did I screw up?"

"Actually, I did. I should have told you how to handle it. It's the first time I've sent you out as an unemployed person. I blew it. I blame the venue. The park. Your shorts. You need to wear longer shorts."

My afterglow was now extinguished. Harper Scott: Mr. Buzzkill.

"What should I have said?"

Harper sighed the way you sigh when you have spent years trying to change someone.

"Okay, you want to write a chapter? Write what I say down and send it to me."

I flipped open my laptop.

"I'm not sure how I got downgraded to stenographer, but go!"

HARPER'S RULES
How to Handle The Compensation Discussion in an Interview

If you are on your first interview and the decision maker asks you how much money you desire, you've witnessed a very clear buying sign. Interviewing 101 says you don't discuss money on the first interview; you know it and they know it. If, knowing this rule, they can't keep from breaking it, it's because they already know at some level they want to hire you and now want to get to the bottom line.

But danger lurks! In my headhunting career, nothing has cost candidates more jobs or money than the wrong response when it comes to the money discussion in an interview.

Here is the age-old dynamic: they want to hire you at the lowest amount possible; you want to get the highest amount possible. Neither one of you wants to feel like you were taken advantage of, and neither one of you wants the other feeling like they were exploited. Both are deeply suspicious that the other is guilty of "fudging" the numbers. (The company says it couldn't possibly pay what you say you want for budgetary reasons, and you say you couldn't possibly accept less due to personal financial commitments.) There is gamesmanship in play here. It's not about money; it's about playing the game well.

"But this isn't a rug at a tag sale," you say, "this is a person's livelihood, a company's bottom line. This shouldn't be trivialized into some puerile notion of one-upmanship. Surely we're all beyond that when it comes to our career!"

Uh, that would be a "no."

Everything is a game, a negotiation. Whether it should be that way is not my concern; my job is to identify the game and win it, for me and my candidates.

Here's the risk: If you answer the seemingly innocent question, "What kind of money are you looking for?" and your answer is too high, the client might assume they can't get you and *never make an offer.*

If your answer is too low, the client *will offer you less* than they would have been willing to pay if pressure were properly applied. So the key is to *stay neutral.* This is wage war, and you are Switzerland.

Neutral Response When Asked About Money

"I am currently at X [your current salary], and looking at a number of opportunities. Right now I'm just interested in pursuing this job and learning more about your company. I'm sure if we get to the offer stage, you will make a fair offer."

Now you can't be trapped. You have established that they are not the only game in town and that others are competing for your talents. You have implied that a reasonable increase will be required without risking overkill.

(If they ask you where else you are interviewing, you may disclose the types of jobs but not the actual companies. Let them know you were asked to keep it confidential and that you are offering everyone the same courtesy.)

"I'm sorry to interrupt," I blurted, "but isn't that a little dicky, Harper? Uh, Harper?"

"I'm sorry, you threw me off. I've never heard the words, 'little dicky' and 'Harper' in the same sentence before."

"Can you hold on, Harper, while I throw up in my mouth?"

"You've tapped into the problem, Casey. An interview is, by design, a weak power dynamic for the candidate: one job, many candidates, and the decision maker is lord and master. Everything I'm telling you serves the larger purpose of shifting the power dynamic. You are there by choice; you want for nothing. It's the only way to play this."

"But that all changes when they make an offer, right?"

"Exactly. Once you've been selected as the person they want, the power dynamic shifts to you. Ready to type some more?"

"Shoot."

Neutral Response (Advanced Version)

Plead the Fifth if pressured. Some companies insist you give them a number. They will press you for a salary that you would find acceptable. The more they push, the harder it is to not yield because you don't want to make them mad. But once you give the number: a) it is hard to change that number, and b) you have lost the leverage of mystery. So, plead the Fifth:

"I can tell you feel strongly about getting an absolute number, and I respect that tremendously as strong leadership that appeals to me, but I just don't have that number finalized. I have other opportunities I need to consider. But I can tell you this (this will satisfy them and titillate, a nice combo): While money is a factor for all of us, and every opportunity I am looking at offers some kind of reasonable increase, my primary motivation is not money. I want to come to work every day with energy and purpose."

"So the message when you say 'some kind of reasonable increase,'" I interjected, "is, 'you will have to pay me more than I'm making to get me,' but at the same time you defuse the avarice stigma. Nice."

"Lucky for you I accept both sincere praise and patronizing flattery."

"Okay, let's get back to me. How can I modify this, considering I am unemployed? And what if I don't have 'other opportunities?'"

"As a temporarily unemployed person, you continue to go back to your last salary as the base number. As for whether or not you actually have other interviews scheduled, that is semantics; you will. Everyone has other opportunities, even if they haven't happened yet. You can still say you are considering them. Going online and reading postings is "considering." You need to be completely honest but not absolutely honest."

"Interesting distinction. Which one are you being right now, Harper?"

"I'm not saying it's how you run your whole life; I'm saying it makes no sense to tell a company you would never interview for any other job because you love them so much and would do anything to work for them. Would you tell someone you were in love with that they could treat you any way they want and you would stay with them no matter what?"

"If we allow for paraphrasing, I think I've said exactly that."

"And how did that work out?"

"Harper, all of this is well and good, but I already told Wallace I wanted a 200K base: 75K higher than the base I had and 200K higher than what I am making now."

"I'll fix it."

"How, without looking dishonest or avaricious?"

"People make new decisions when faced with new information. I presented you new information which makes those numbers no longer applicable, and Wallace will have to make a new decision."

"I love it when you talk spin."

"First I need to know how you left things with Wallace."

"We agreed to meet on the 17th at their Manhattan office at 9 A.M. He wants me to meet the other managing partners and get a product demo."

I knew this would please Harper. He has prepped me so many times for interviews that it has become reflexive for me to follow his Cardinal Rule of Ending Interviews.

Harper's Rule: Never leave an interview without closing on the next step in the process. Don't leave without a date and time for the next interview.

He even gave me a script and told me to memorize it so that it would sound spontaneous:

"Wallace, I appreciate how generous you've been with your time, and I'm impressed by you and the organization. Based on what you've shared with me and what I've done in my career, I think I can make an immediate and significant contribution and would like very much to pursue this. What's your schedule like?"

"You may not be going on the 17th," Harper said offhandedly. "I'll get back to you on that."

"That's your fix? Cancelling my only interview?"

"Yes, because the new information that requires you to change your compensation requirements is that you have two other companies who want to see you for similar positions, and you don't want to make any commitments without hearing everyone out, this being such a career watershed for you and all."

"But I don't have two other interviews! I don't want to bluff, Harper."

"I know, I wish you'd work on that. Don't worry, I have two other companies I want to send you to, and I will use this fact to make it clear to Wallace that he will have to up the ante to attract you."

I felt a pout coming on. I was not getting my way. That's never good for anyone near me. I am a world-class pout.

"Harper, I want that job! I am going on the 17th!"

"Casey, it's a strategy. You *will* get another meeting with Wallace. But we need to do it out of strength. And what if you don't get the offer? What if they hire someone else?"

"He loved me, Harper. We connected. I know he wants to hire me."

How could I explain this to rational, emotionally detached Harper? He is writing a book about the analogy of relationships to work, and he doesn't understand one of the most central parallels: I am a one-man woman.

I don't want any more interviews. I love Wallace, he loves me, and we are meant to be together. It already feels like cheating on him to go on other interviews.

"Harper, I just want this to be all over." Suddenly my throat hurt.

"I get it. You want to cut a deal with Wallace right now, go on your date with Peter Bonetti tomorrow, and wake up Monday morning with a new commute and a ring on your left hand."

"See, in my head it seemed hopeful and romantic. When you say it, it sounds crazy and pathetic."

"It is neither, but that's not how it works. Look, I want you to go to work for Wallace, but I want you to get the best possible deal because you'll be living with it a long time; and remember, I've got money at stake here, too! A little trust, please."

I was being tested. I wanted so much to take him down, to let him know I knew he wasn't charging Wallace a fee for me. "Funny you say that. Wallace asked me if I trusted you."

It was nice to see Harper, if not thrown, at least a little out of balance, if only for a moment.

"He did? I don't . . . why would he ask that? How did that come up?"

To be fair, he didn't specifically ask me if I trusted Harper. We were already an hour into the interview. Wallace asked pointed and savvy questions about the sales process, the nuances of the product mix, and the market realities that were in play in each of the verticals. It was a detailed and technical examination of my experience. And then, out of the blue, he said, "So who do you trust, Casey?"

I could think of several responses that would have satisfied him and served me well. But something about this kind and thoughtful man made me want to be straight with him. Being around Harper made you want to try harder, but being around Wallace Avery made you want to be better.

"I'm sorry to say no one comes to mind. I don't give up trust very easily, Wallace."

This seemed to sadden him. I could tell he genuinely wished what I had just said was not true. Then he gave me a smile that surely killed in his day.

"Well, perhaps I will make it a goal to become someone you trust. I would like that."

"Whoa, that is a lofty ambition, Wallace. But it's good to have goals, right?"

Wallace laughed and looked away. He was at that wonderful stage attractive older men get to where they are still skilled at flirting even though they are harmless. Why does our skin have to dry and fall and crease in order for us to get comfortable living in it?

"I would have thought," Wallace said, "given his largesse regarding his fee, that you would have said you trusted Harper."

"Harper has never given me a reason not to trust him."

"But that doesn't mean you do."

"Do you have some issue with Harper, Wallace?"

"Absolutely not. Dealt with him for years, always done right by me. He's just a really clever guy with access to a lot of sensitive company information. People more clever than me make me wary."

"For what it's worth, I think Harper knows where to draw the boundaries."

Wallace nodded vigorously. "Agreed. Anyway, with what he's been through recently, I've been impressed with how he's handled himself and how he's stayed focused on the job. A very disciplined guy."

What he's been through? Recently? What did he mean? Was Wallace implying Harper had to overcome something? Personal? Business? Wallace saw the same look on my face he saw in the grill room. He knew I had no idea what he was referring to.

"I see I'm talking out of school again. And I hate when people do that to me. So what say we get back on point? Casey, I can't get into the specifics right now, but the timing for whoever gets this position is pretty fortuitous. Some very big, very fundamental changes in capital and investment are happening behind the scenes, and that's all I can say."

He was clearly referring to the Cisco takeover. Harper mentioned a 2 billion dollar infusion. I knew enough to keep my mouth shut, but I need to work on my poker face.

"Something tells me you know what I'm referring to," Wallace said dryly. "Did our friend bring you up to speed?"

Time to ruin this whole deal or hit one out of the park. If I'm going down, I'm going to go down feeling good about myself.

"Wallace, with all due respect, if he did, I wouldn't tell you. He would have told me in confidence, and once someone tells me something in confidence then it's in the vault. If I violated that trust, how would you ever be able to trust me with information you want in the vault?"

"I wouldn't," Wallace said.

"So, maybe I'll make you trusting me a goal of mine, too."

"It's good to have goals. Casey, I would be pleased if you would come back to meet some of the key players on the board. Are you available on the 17th to come into Manhattan for the day?"

Something to hold back that says I'm different . . . Time to bring it.

"That depends, Wallace."

"On what?"

"Who do I get to sell to first?"

Wallace sat back. It didn't matter whether he realized at some level that Harper might have fed me his question, he still was used to asking it, and he still wanted to know my answer.

"Who would you want to sell to first?"

"There was a great quote in *Slate* magazine's technology section a few months ago. 'Everyone is intoxicated about how social networking is bringing about change, but no one is noticing that it is not making anyone a red cent.' That seemed a trenchant comment to me."

"I believe I wrote that article."

"I believe you did. And you're right. So here's what I think. We don't try to sell to consumers. We don't try to take down Facebook. We get Walmart or the NFL, or any large enterprise, and we tell them we will provide them with their own social network, a network of customers, vendors, and employees. Connect them to their own world and leave the outside world out. The way to make money in social networking is for the network to become an entity's primary way of marketing—a way to create its own culture."

Wallace nodded, and the hair stood up on the back of my neck.

"So," he said, "we don't get into the ad revenue wars?"

"We are a fee-based service. The ads are intrinsic in the very idea of the network. We take both."

I threw my hair back and started to gather my things. Leave them wanting more. Harper said, "Leave an interview on your own terms."

"Anyway, just a thought," I said, standing up. "I don't want to waste your time coming back if my ideas are contrary to your plan. I'm sure you know best . . ."

". . . and then, Wallace said, 'Consider the 17th booked, consider me behind the concept, and consider me duly impressed with you . . .' I hear tapping, Harper. Are you actually emailing while I am sharing my conversation with your client?"

"Did he actually say he was behind the concept?"

"Verbatim. So you see? I have to go on the 17th."

"I'll do what I can and be back to you. You need to get ready for your date."

God! My date! I had spent so much energy being "on" for Wallace, and now dealing with the life-sucking force that is Harper, I just wanted to stay home and veg.

"Did you do your homework on him, Casey? Same principles, remember?"

"No, I did not. I thought I'd try an innovative method and have an actual conversation with him during the actual date."

"I figured, so I did it for you. There's something you need to know about this guy. Turns out—"

"Harper, stop. I will defer to your judgment on my livelihood. But just because I am divorced and you are married, just because you have a theory about work and love, I will not have you doing investigative work on the men I date."

"So you don't want to know?"

"Of course I want to know. But I am going to choose to not know. I am going to go on this date with an open mind, and I am not going to let you ruin that for me."

"For the record, it's really juicy stuff. I would want to know."

"Harper."

"What?"

I wanted to say something indignant. Or go the other way and be funny. But my throat was closing. My eyes were doing that stupid, welling-up thing.

"I'm lonely. You know?"

"Yeah. I do. Go on your date. I'll deal with Wallace. Enjoy yourself."

CHAPTER EIGHT

DATING IS LIKE INTERVIEWING . . . ONLY HARDER

My burst of integrity with Harper lasted about two hours. I was so proud of myself for making the right, if utterly romantic choice, and not accepting Harper's intel on Peter's past, and then I got two text messages. One, from Harper, was heartening; he had spoken to Wallace, reworked the compensation expectations, and said I could plan on the 17th. The second text was from Peter.

"Exactly what is 'smart casual'?"

Sigh. In my experience with men, the correct answer to this is, "Not what you were thinking of wearing." But it was way too early in our relationship for honesty, so I answered that I was sure whatever he was thinking was fine.

His return text: "That's good, since I don't own a jacket. Are you wearing jeans?"

Harper always says that his clients decide within the first thirty to ninety seconds in an interview if they are going to hire you, and the rest of the entire interview process, even if it takes hours and several visits, is just filler, their way of reassuring themselves of the decision they had already unconsciously made. I remembered what I had written to Harper:

Dress up for the interview even if you know it's a casual work environment. It shows respect, confidence, and attitude. It covers your weaknesses.

I was deciding from a text, without even seeing what Peter was going to wear, that this was not going to work out.

So now that I knew I was wearing jeans, I chose a plain white silk blouse that buttoned in front and a tweed jacket that made me look hot in an academic way. Now, the tough call. On a first date, there is always the question of cleavage. I left the top two buttons unbuttoned in an attempt to punish Peter for his text messages, and then I looked to see if my breasts, not crazy large but full, and long a trademark advantage, had sagged. Breast implants have become so common nowadays that now I feel like a company who has lost its patent rights and is now competing with copycats and cheap imitators.

My Blackberry beeped. Peter again.

"Do you want me to pick you up?"

Oh no. I need to be able to bail if things go to hell in a hurry. I replied that I would meet him there.

Another beep.

"Is there parking on the street or do you have to pay the valet?"

I found myself wondering what I would do when the check came. I have made more money in a year than Peter will make in four or five as a personal trainer, so I should probably insist on paying, or at least pay half. And yet, I am resentful. I am. the. girl. I expect him to pay. Is that awful? Fine, I'm awful then, so why am I going?

Send a top candidate to a top company and they will love each other. Send a top candidate to a crummy company and the company will hate him/her. Send a crummy candidate to a crummy company and they love each other. People and companies are not created equal and must be matched accordingly.

I'm starting to think I am a top candidate and Peter is a crummy company.

So why don't I cancel? I need more ammunition.

Harper said he had information on Peter that I should know before I went on the date. I couldn't call Harper and ask him; I couldn't give him that satisfaction. But I could find out for myself.

What I love about Google is its fairness. If I were looking for a black dress for a party and I searched Google, and Jennifer Lopez, sitting in the presidential suite of the Palm Beach Ritz Carlton, put in the same search string, we would both get the same results.

I searched under Peter's full name. Then the gym . . . certified personal trainers . . . the government's "most wanted" list . . . registered sex offenders. In a momentary lapse of blind hope, I searched for Mensa membership. Then the blogs . . . Not a single entry having anything to do with Peter. Google sucks!

When I am stressed or fear an outcome, my mind drifts. When I couldn't find out anything about Peter, I started running Google searches on Harper. I found the usual stuff: his company's website propaganda, a *Wall Street Journal* interview Harper had done a year or so ago, his profile under the gaudy title of "40 under 40, The Top Corporate Headhunters in America."

Then I saw the search result from *Connecticut Magazine*. The Scott home was featured, well over a year ago, as one of "New England's finest homes." When I pulled up the link, there was a picture of Harper and his wife, Maggie. Even with the poor quality of the computer reproduction, she was exquisite. She is not only a size four after having a child, but she has curves and angles just where you are supposed to. She was too beautiful to hate.

I Googled Maggie. MBA from the University of Chicago . . . Columbia undergrad and law school—two graduate degrees! She worked as an immigration lawyer in the city for three years and gave it up to do social service work. She was named to MACY (the Mayor's Advisory Committee on Youth) in Manhattan. Okay, I take it back, nobody is too beautiful to hate. I'm going on my date.

I was about to exit my browser when I noticed one more entry about her MACY commitment, and that's when I saw it: "Margaret Carlson-Scott says new membership drive . . ."

It was the only entry where she had hyphenated her name. Now why would she do that? Why now? I went back over the other entries. Nope. No hyphen, just Maggie or Margaret Scott.

The only two times in my life I had to deal with the "to hyphenate or not to hyphenate" dilemma were 1) when I got married to Donald and 2) when I divorced him. For me, as a professional salesperson who was established in my niche, the decision was easy, since my maiden name was hard to pronounce and even harder to spell. I wanted my contacts to recognize me.

So why is Maggie suddenly using it? All I could think of was Wallace telling me Harper had "been through a lot" recently. I was instantly convinced that Harper was separated or divorced. For all I knew, Harper was the villain and she had caught him red handed. Maybe Harper is a terrible and distant dad.

No, no way. Harper softens visibly whenever he mentions Jess; she is his world. But how would I know? Harper puts a wall up; he makes you feel like you are on intimate terms, but it's a one-way street. He is intimate with you; you are never intimate with him.

Stop it, Casey. You have a date with a perfectly nice guy.

I used to make Donald promise me we would never become one of the married couples we would see in nice restaurants all the time. The scary ones were those who had simply become so tired of each other that conversation and entertainment were beside the point, which was to get out of the house and not have to cook.

But as I walked into the restaurant to meet Peter, I longed to be one of those couples. At least they didn't have butterflies in their stomachs, didn't stare at themselves in the mirror from every conceivable angle, didn't shave in long-neglected areas—just in case.

I saw him at the adjacent bar. He gave me a nervous smile and attempted a hapless sort of wave. I suddenly realized why I liked him. It wasn't the hard body or the full lips or the thick, black hair and olive skin—Peter was melancholy. But . . . after propping Donald up for so long, why did I want someone fragile?

Peter stood up and reached out his arms, signaling an embrace and sparing me the agony of choice, and whispered "so glad you're here" into my ear as he pulled back.

I pride myself on taking control at the beginning of a date with a witty remark or a wry observation, but I had nothing. I wondered if I had a goofy smile on my face. I have been many things to please men, but I draw the line at a goofy smile.

There were two glasses of wine at the bar.

"Cakebread Merlot. I'm not even going to pretend to know the year. But that's what you like, right?"

"Um, okay, yes. I do. How do you know that?"

"I notice you talk to Janet at the gym. She is tight with Nina, who teaches the Body Attack. She put me in touch with Hannah, who told me she has been your drinking buddy long enough to know and recommended Cakebread Merlot."

"Well, I hope she was buddy enough to tell you I'm not that particular, especially when it comes to dating."

"Oh." Peter became eight years old in an instant.

"No, I don't mean I'm not particular about who I date, I . . . Okay, let's go with this: I love the wine, Peter, and it was very thoughtful. Thanks."

"Cheers." He appeared to be back to his age and happy. I'm dating Tom Hanks in *Big*.

Just when I thought I would go off-script with Peter, he reached into his surprisingly high-quality black cashmere sports jacket, set off with jeans and grey pullover, held up his cell phone, and shut it off.

"Now that you're here, I have no need for this for the night."

This was a gallant gesture, a way of showing me I had his complete attention. But while I would never go into an interview with my cell phone on, this was a first date. And a cell phone is how a girl gets out of a disaster, the dating equivalent of pepper spray.

But Peter put his phone down on the bar, completing his gesture, and rested it near mine. I had to either match Peter or lose face. I decided to lose face. I have a good feeling about this guy, but I have been wrong before. (After all, he claimed he had no jacket!) I left my phone on.

If Harper was right about the symmetry between interviewing and dating, and since I had just killed on my interview, I merely needed to remember his rules for first meetings.

We all like to talk about ourselves.

Be truly present and really listening.

Don't bring up negatives, and don't talk about your ex (spouse or job).

This shouldn't be difficult. I knew little about Peter, so I thought I'd start with his family. But I never got the chance. Peter took a Budweiser-sized sip of Cakebread and launched in.

"You wouldn't be a rebound."

"Excuse me?"

"Well, I know everyone always says that rebounds never work out. And I did, full disclosure, go through a really horrible breakup, but the point is I have had a few dates since, and so, technically, this wouldn't be a rebound."

"Okay," I said, in the voice I used when the guy in Union Square tells me I need to prepare for Judgment Day.

"Although my friends, Hank and Debbie, they were like, total rebound, like they met two days after the people they broke up with moved out, and that was two years ago, and they have a baby and are completely happy, and so who knows, right? So rebounds don't scare me, and kids don't scare me either. Do you want kids?"

"Peter, when you turned off your phone, did you turn off your filter?"

"My filter?"

"Yes, you have to have a filter. You, in one fell swoop, broke every rule of what not to talk about on first dates. Maybe Harper's right; there really is a market out there."

"Who's Harper?"

"Doesn't matter. Peter, we don't even have our table yet. We should be deciding on tap water or sparkling, discussing food allergies. You can't ask me if I want kids."

"Okay," he said, nodding somberly. "I'm going to check on our table."

"Good."

He got halfway to the hostess and turned around. He stood in front of me for a moment and then placed his hand on my neck and kissed me. It was a really good kiss.

"I don't have food allergies," he said.

I shrugged. "I've got nothing against kids. In the abstract."

Know your objective. The objective is to be asked back for a second interview or for another date.

At that moment, I would have told you a second date was a lock, an engagement a foregone conclusion, and a twenty-fifth anniversary party thrown at the home of our most successful child a distinct possibility. But the rush I felt after Peter kissed me was about to be tempered. Hannah had suggested lunch for just this reason. "Even if he's got game, you can't expect him to have three hours of game!" she said. She was right. From the moment we sat down, we began to unravel.

At first I was tolerant. Peter asked me about my work and when I told him I was on severance, he had no clue what that meant. When I explained, he shook his head and said, "I'd be scared out of my mind if I was unemployed."

He isn't dumb, Casey. He's just not from your world, that's all.

But before I could change the subject, Peter told me the only other person he knew in sales was his friend Artie, who sold cars. Peter said he could never be "pushy or aggressive, trying to talk someone into paying for options they don't need and stuff. But hey," he said, "Artie makes good money."

I should have reached for the cell phone, but the ugly side of me was making her way from my brain to my lips.

"How much money does Artie make?"

"He said he made over a hundred grand one year. Not last year but one year."

"I've averaged between 220 and 350K a year for the last five years. I'm not pushy or manipulative. Ever hear of ROI?"

Peter sadly shook his head.

"Didn't think so." I needed to either stop talking or leave. The waitress rescued me by noticing our empty glasses.

"Would you like to order some wine?"

"Sure. We were having the Cakebread Merlot," Peter said.

"You might want to consider the Sonoma since you're having the lamb, or if you'd prefer, I can send over the sommelier."

"Okay," Peter said brightly, "we'll have the Sommelier. Is that a red?"

The waitress looked at me helplessly, and I said the Sonoma was fine. My sister would not be surprised by the evening so far. "When you date men with money, you try and compete with them, which turns them off," she says, "and when you date men who don't make a lot of money, you claim they're boring or not smart, when really you just don't respect them."

"I feel like I'm maybe trying too hard," Peter said. "Sorry."

Peter looked forlorn, so I tried to regroup.

"So let me tell you about the love of my life," I began, "my source of daily and unconditional love: Starbucks, my Maine Coon cat."

I have several stock Starbucks stories that are adorable even to the non–cat lover. Not many people realize how large Maine Coons can get (males up to twenty-eight pounds, females up to eighteen), how beautiful and regal they become, how affectionate and smart they are, and how long they live (up to twenty-four years if kept inside religiously). I started one of my stock, can't-miss, Starbucks-wins-in-the-end stories.

"I'm allergic to cats. Most of them, anyway. Dogs too. But I hear there are medications I could take."

Okay, check please. And I'll take the Sonoma to go. While I would have probably pretended my phone was on vibrate and claimed that I heard it go off, it actually did go off. I dug in my purse and told Peter I was sorry, but I had to take this.

"You don't even know who it is yet," he said brusquely.

True, and it was rude and obvious of me—and I didn't care. I pulled out the phone and had to fight not to smile. It was Harper.

"Hi," I said.

"Well, that answers that."

"What?"

"You picked up, which means you needed to be rescued."

I excused myself, held up a finger indicating I'd be just a wee bit, and wandered until I found an alcove between the ladies' room and the kitchen.

"Harper, I need to know what you found about Peter."

"Why? So you can use it as an excuse to end the evening?"

"Maybe. Give."

"Hmm, I don't think so. You made that call. Live with it."

"Harper, do not mess with me."

"Hold on, I need to write this down as I tell it to you. This is one of my rules that applies to both dating and interviewing."

HARPER'S RULE
Find a Graceful Way Out

If you find yourself in an interview or date where your gut tells you not to pursue, but you lack the courage to come clean—and so then create a graceful way out by justifying it with some logical, unimpeachable reason— you are being unfair to both yourself and the person or entity you are with.

"But Harper, he ordered the sommelier."

"I've met the sommelier there; he's very attractive. I hear he's married, though, note to Peter."

"It's not just that; we're different. I can see it already. As my headhunter, as a self-proclaimed believer that the rules of interviewing and dating are parallel, tell me: do people last longer in careers if they share a common set of sensibilities with their co-workers, or are they happier if they are opposite?"

"Opposites do attract," he said, "but it is strictly short term. It fades."

"Tell me what you learned about Peter so I can make an informed decision here."

"Okay, you win. Keep in mind I heard this from two sources and then verified it with someone official enough to know."

Peter tapped me on the shoulder, and I was so focused on trying to hear Harper amid the din of the restaurant, I whirled and gave him an angry look. He stepped back.

"I wasn't trying to interrupt you or anything," he said. "I was going in the men's room, right behind you, and they did bring the lamb a while ago, and well, it is kind of quiet at the table."

I mouthed the words "so sorry," held up the phone, and rolled my eyes.

"Look, I have to go," I said loudly, making a big show for Peter.

"Yes, the *Silence of the Lambs*. I heard, Clarice."

I decided to hit back as Peter entered the men's room.

"How is it you are calling me on a Saturday night? Where's your family?"

"Do you want to know what I know or don't you?" he said, his voice curt.

"Go."

"Peter's ex, not his wife but a woman he lived with for quite some time, filed a restraining order against him. He was ordered to stay 500 feet away from her at all times."

Peter came out of the men's room and walked toward me. He was approximately 495 feet closer than the person who knew him best petitioned the law to allow.

"Casey, did you hear me?" Harper said.

I flipped my cell shut.

I'm sure my therapist would have a field day with the fact that Harper's revelation made the rest of the dinner so much more fun. How do we expect to rid the world of evil when it adds so much energy and is so much less boring than good things? But we'll never know because I won't tell her. My main goal in therapy is to make her laugh. She laughs once, and I feel I'm making progress.

Suddenly Peter was fascinating to me. What did he do that justified a restraining order? Did he break things? Glassware? Jaws? This man needed to be restrained! I found this very sexy. After all, Donald had been restrained all the time; I needed to file an *unleashing* order on him. I couldn't take my eyes off Peter. I started to feel warm. I noticed that his plate was empty and mine had hardly been touched.

"So, how can you eat like this and drink wine and have the body from hell?" I asked.

He said he worked out three hours a day and I asked him why. He said it made him feel better.

Years earlier, when I asked Harper the same question, he said being strong made him feel strong and seem strong to others. It was a control thing with Harper. Peter's way seemed so much more pure.

The end of a date or an interview is always awkward. Will we ever see each other again? Are we being polite as we tell each other we enjoyed meeting each other, or have we connected in some real way? As we stood waiting for the valet to bring my car around, Peter broke the rules again.

HARPER'S RULE
Be Prepared for but Never Expect an Offer on the First Interview

If a company offers you the job after the first interview, it could be love at first sight, the timing is perfect, and you have found the ideal job. But more likely it is a warning sign that there is something wrong with the job and they want your commitment before you figure it out. The fact that they are willing to commit to you without knowing much about you should scare you. Tell them you are flattered but would like to come back and learn more about the opportunity. If this is unacceptable to them, walk away knowing you have dodged a bullet.

"Just so you know," he began, "as tentative and as lame as I was at having dinner in a place like this, that's how good I am at having sex."

"You must be *really* good at having sex, then."

"So," he began, his voice rising as he went, "is there still like, a three-date rule before having sex?"

I had a moment to gather myself because the valet brought the car around, and then he kissed me again. Slow as syrup.

"I am unaware of any set rules," I said. "Why don't you get your car and follow me?"

The moment Peter turned away, I took out my cell, scrolled to the last call, and pressed the SEND button.

"So when you say 'a restraining order,' can you be more specific?"

"Sure," Harper said calmly, "it's what I'm thinking about getting against you for next Saturday night."

"Come on, Harper, there is a broad spectrum. Did he take the lawn furniture because they used his credit card, or am I taking my life into my hands here?"

"Things have obviously improved since we last spoke."

"Gotta tell you, Harper, I don't read restraining order. He's a sweet, sweet guy with the tiniest little round butt."

"So what do you want from me? Permission?"

"I don't need your permission to do anything, Harper Scott."

"Then why are we on the phone?"

"He is without guile, Harper. It really is amazing. I didn't think such people existed. I am about to go home with a man without guile."

"So, a court looks at evidence and decides a woman's safety is at risk and legally restrains a man from coming near her, and you not only take him home, but judge him to be without guile. Quite a trick. Oh wait, can you trick someone and still be without guile?"

"You know what I think, Harper? I think she filed the restraining order to hurt him. I think by accusing him publicly of something he was incapable of, she thought he might stay."

"That's a nice theory. I hope for your sake you're right."

And the phone went dead. I walked over to Peter's car and he opened the door to get out, but I closed it and motioned for him to roll down the window. I leaned in and kissed him.

"I'm going to go home. By myself. I hope you call me. I hope we get to do something a little less stuffy. Thanks, I had a great night."

As I walked to my car, Peter called out to me. "Did I do something wrong?"

"Nope. But there are rules."

CHAPTER NINE

THE FOLLOW-UP PROTOCOL TO INTERVIEWS AND DATES

They say when you are about to die—careening off the guardrail, let's say—that everything slows down. People who survive such things talk about their lives passing before their eyes.

Being unemployed is pretty much the same way, except you don't wake up surrounded by loved ones telling you how lucky you are. They either assume you are trying to get a job and shouldn't be bothered, or they think calling you is too risky in case unemployment is airborne.

By Tuesday, three days after my interview, and two days after my date: a) I had no call or correspondence from InterAnnex or Wallace Avery; b) I had no call, email, or text from Peter; c) I had nothing from Harper—no information, no book chapter, nothing.

As I walked back from my bill-stuffed mailbox, my cell phone went off.

She said her name was Leena, a "colleague" of Harper's, and he had asked her to follow up with me since he'd received "several" messages from me about the status with InterAnnex.

"Why isn't Harper calling me himself?"

"He is out of the office."

"Leena. Harper is connected to his PDA like it's a respirator."

"Ms. Matthews, I've been here four years, and I'm a senior associate; the information he wanted to pass on to you is standard protocol for us."

Translation: stop being a diva and let me help you get a job.

Leena next informed me that the information was also part of Mr. Scott's "publish-ing project."

"Do tell."

"Very well."

HARPER'S RULES FOR THANK-YOU NOTES

The first thing you should do is send a thank-you note to the primary decision maker. This note should be handwritten and should be sent direct mail.

1. It should be no more than two paragraphs.
2. It should be personal as well as professional.
3. It shouldn't be frivolous or cute.
4. It should never be a card.
5. If your handwriting is illegible, a printed Word document is fine as long as you sign the postscript and fold it neatly into the correct-sized envelope.
6. If you absolutely cannot handwrite a note, email is an acceptable backup.
7. You should also thank, in separate emails, anyone else you may have met.
8. Always end with a positive message about pursuing the position.

"If you would permit me, Ms. Matthews, here is an example for InterAnnex that you can feel free to use or modify:

Dear Mr. Wallace Avery:

I just wanted to take a moment to thank you for the time you spent with me on Friday. It was obvious to me why InterAnnex is such a successful company and why under your dynamic leadership it will continue to grow. I appreciated your candor, humor, and professionalism.

Having had some time to reflect, I feel my background and the duties and challenges you described are an excellent match, and I look forward to discussing this in more detail. Thanks for the gift of your time.

Sincerely,

"Ms. Matthews, did you get all that? Did I go too fast?"

"Amazingly, I managed to keep up. Do you know my background, Leena?"

"I haven't reviewed it specifically . . ."

"Do you really think I don't know that I am supposed to send a handwritten thank-you letter?"

"So you already sent one to Mr. Avery?"

"Well, no, actually . . . You know what, Leena? Why don't you tell Harper that I will deal directly with Mr. Avery from this point forward, and he can stay on his writing sabbatical, or wherever he is."

"That wouldn't be wise, Ms. Matthews. In fact, that is the next part of the protocol Mr. Scott asked me to review with you. Ready?"

HARPER'S RULE
We Want What Is Difficult to Get

Never contact the hiring authority after your first interview.

Even if you are not working through a headhunter, other than sending a thank-you note, any followup attempting to show interest in the job or to move the process faster only *weakens* your position.

Right, like all those voice mails from Peter trying to get me to go out with him. I finally go out with him and three days later he suddenly has reclaimed his dignity. Such is my effect on men.

This can be difficult, of course, and frustrating, especially if the company promised to get back to you by a certain time or date. But keep in mind, it is not necessarily a reflection of their interest in you, and you must not take it personally. You must trust they haven't forgotten you and the impact you made in the interview.

The next move is for you, in a separate communication from your thank-you note, to send three references with contact information to the person who interviewed you. Email is the preferred mode. You should also include a salary history.

Make sure you "preload" your references. Even though they may have told you when you left your previous company or companies that they would give you a positive reference, it is in your interest to call them and let them know you had a successful interview, give them the name of who would be calling to check your reference, and ask them without equivocation to recommend you for the position. Describe the position for them at length, forward them a link to the company's website, and ask them to peruse it before they get the call.

Okay, I need to do that. Damn, I'm starting to like Leena. She is a sharp kid and she knows her stuff.

"But, Leena, in my case, I assume Harper has already given my references to Wallace."

"Oh, yes. I see a note attached that says they were sent last week and that Mr. Avery wanted to call them personally himself."

"That's a good sign, right? Leena?"

"Not always. It could also mean he had some concern about you that he wanted to hear either confirmed or denied directly from your references."

Harper, I think your protégé here is going to do just fine. She is evil, and yet I like her.

"Well, Mr. Scott and Mr. Avery said I had a meeting on the 17th. Is that confirmed? Come on, Leena, give!"

"No. It is not."

No one has died, I told myself. Yet I could hardly breathe.

Had Harper taught Leena the "Take It Away"?

HARPER'S RULE
The "Take It Away"

If done correctly, the "Take It Away" will identify who has the upper hand. It must be succinct, matter-of-fact, and with no qualifiers. Deliver the "Take It Away" and get off the phone.

The "Take It Away" only works if you hang up. If you don't, you *dilute* the message and you lose. Done correctly, the "Take It Away" is jarring to recipients, making them realize they have waited too long or negotiated too hard, and now will lose what they suddenly realize they *must* have.

Harper would call me on this in a second. Here goes, Leena . . .

"Leena, I'm not comfortable. Mr. Avery said the 17th, and Harper knows my credentials are impeccable. If they can't commit to the date they asked me to reserve, I withdraw my candidacy. Please tell Harper."

And I hung up. I hope you're right, Harper.

I decided I was on a "Take it Away" roll. I went to the gym, after a very minor make-up prep of just over an hour.

I envisioned a saunter. The area where the personal trainers take their clients through their paces with things like Bosu balls and body bars is adjacent to the cardio area, and if he was in there torturing someone in the name of fitness, I would acknowledge him with my eyes but not smile, and then "saunter" by him.

My plan unraveled immediately. Peter was on his knees on one of the yoga mats and leaning back as if he were in a game of tug of war. But instead of a rope, he was pulling the leg of a woman lying on the mat below him. Then he pushed her bent leg back toward her chest, fully stretching her hamstring and exposing her glutes. Not a trace of cellulite. My saunter, which had begun so promisingly in the parking lot, came to a screeching halt.

I turned away, smiled as brightly at his slutty client as I could, and as I sat down on a LifeCycle, Leena's number flashed on my cell.

"Hi, Leena."

"Ms. Matthews, just wanted to get back to you. I couldn't get ahold of Mr. Scott, so I took it upon myself to call InterAnnex, speak to Mr. Avery directly, and formally withdraw you from consideration."

Damn! It backfired! Enjoy yourself, Casey, when you have to sign up for unemployment.

"You did?" I managed, meekly.

"Of course I didn't. I just had to get back at you for using the 'Take It Away' on me. By the time I realized you were using my own training on me, I had completely freaked out and called Mr. Scott."

"Leena, did you just punk me?"

"Maybe a little."

Okay, I love her. I started to laugh, which made her laugh, and the moment would have gone on a bit if Peter hadn't come around the corner.

"Uh, sorry, I'll talk to you when you're done."

"No you won't. I'm going to be a while, and then I'm going to work out. I'm going to tell you one of the great rules of business, but I've been convinced recently that the rules of life and love are no different. Here's the rule: 'Time Kills Deals.'"

I settled back on the LifeCycle and gave Leena my full attention.

"Whoa, that sounded cold," she said. "Can I ask?"

"A guy I went out with Friday. No contact since. Just ran into him."

"Ouch. But maybe something happened. Maybe he couldn't reach out. Maybe he had a family thing—"

"Leena, listen to me. 'Yes' is great. 'No' is fine. 'Maybe' doesn't work. Understand?"

"Um, hold on. Mr. Scott is on the other line. I'm going to conference him in."

"Casey," Harper said, "I hear you're abusing my staff."

"I didn't say that," Leena interjected.

"The 'Take It Away,' by the way, was well played."

Harper didn't sound right; he was slightly hoarse.

"Harper, I'll ask you what I asked Leena, who incidentally, is great: What is the concern Wallace Avery has about me that is jeopardizing me getting that job?"

"Who says there is one?"

"Leena, are you recording this call? I'm about to help your boss write one of his chapters. Ready, Harper?"

He sighed. I'd never heard him sound tired before.

HARPER'S RULES
Time Kills Deals

This theory is based on some simple notions:
When we truly want something we act.
The longer we wait the more "life variables" we allow.
There is no such thing as 'I don't have time' in the modern world.

"You want to do the honors on the first one, Casey?"

I was happy to jump in. I believed in it utterly. If I had waited passively for my customers to call back when they promised they would, I would never have made my quota, let alone become a top producer.

"Leena, you just found out you have a formal party to attend tonight. You go right to the mall because this is the only window of time you have to buy a black dress. A woman comes up to you in the store, sees you browsing and says, 'Can I help you?' What do you say?"

"I would say, 'No thanks, just looking.'"

"Right. And that would be a lie. You are, in fact, desperate to have a black dress as soon as possible. Why don't you admit your situation to the salesperson? Because resistance to being persuaded is a given. We push back, even when we want or need something."

"Every time I call people who have résumés on Monster," Leena said, "and tell them about a job, they tell me they're not sure they're really looking for a job, even though their résumé is on a job board."

"Every time I get asked out," I said, "I always say I'm busy for whatever night they first suggest, and I make them find a different night."

"Luckily," Harper said, "resistance is no match for desire. When we want something or someone, our senses begin to work sporadically. We think about the object of our desire. Our resistance reminds us to go slow, but all we can see are the possibilities.

"Leena, you and Mark bought a house recently, right?"

Leena is married? She sounds like she can't be more than twenty-four. And they have a house?

"When did you know you wanted the house?"

"Oh God, the first walk-through. Once I saw the chestnut floors, the wallpaper in the baby's room . . ."

And she has a baby? Mark Junior at twenty-four . . . I am a total loser.

"And even though you told the realtor you were going to think about it and look at some other options, you and Mark began crunching numbers in the car."

"Actually, I begged the realtor not to show it to anyone else until I had a chance to work on Mark."

"Your resistance was being told by your desire that 'Time Kills Deals.' And when did you make the offer?"

"Later that day."

"And did they accept it?"

"No. They counteroffered. After a long, excruciating day."

"One day is not long, but it seemed long because you wanted it. And how long before you countered successfully?"

"Oh, God," Leena laughed, "twenty minutes. Thirty years of payments decided in twenty minutes."

"You did nothing wrong. When we want something, we act."

Peter was at the juice bar counter munching on a Power Bar. If he wanted me, I wouldn't have had to humiliate myself and come to the gym to show him I wasn't interested. His natural *resistance* to being hurt would have been no match for his *desire*.

Harper was still going:

HARPER'S RULES
Time Kills Deals, Part Two

The longer we wait, the more life variables we allow. The excuses we all make seem harmless:

'I just want to think about it.'

'It's a big decision, so I want to be sure.'

'If it's the right thing to do, it will be right next week.'

It takes guts for us to see this for what it is: fear of change. In my career as a headhunter, as well as in my entire existence as a friend or colleague to people making relationship choices, the thing that is most astonishing to me is how often—

"—we continue to do the things and stay with the people we already know are wrong for us. Sorry, Harper. I've heard you say this before, and I get it now." He continued:

The real problem is when we feel we *will* make the change, but we just need some time 'to get used to the idea.' Let's look at the life variables that can occur while we're mustering the courage to act. Here's what happens in my office all the time. We get a candidate an offer that pays him twelve percent more than he currently makes. The benefits are better, with a better match on his 401(k). He goes in a controller, but the VP of finance is retiring in two years, so his promotional path is clear. What does he do when he gets his offer?

"You're saying even this guy says he wants to think about it?" Leena said.

"You say that now, Leena, but you've been out of school for less than two years. He has been with his company for ten years. His boss hired him; he admires the man and dreads disappointing him. He complains about the commute, but he has gotten used to having time to unwind after work before coming home and dealing with his young kids. He has friends at his job.

"And deep inside, despite all the obvious reasons why he should and probably will act, he is worried that he will be exposed as not being the excellent performer he has sold himself as, and he has nightmares about being called in two weeks into the job and being released for being an imposter."

"That is so sad," I lamented.

"An editor of *Parade Magazine* said the one question he could ask any celebrity, no matter how arrogant, that nails them instantly, was, 'What are you going to do when they figure out who you really are?'"

"But ultimately he takes the job, right?" Leena said.

"Perhaps. But he's rolling the dice with the life variables in the interim."

Harper was right about Leena: at twenty-four, life was black and white, and the people wallowing in grisaille seemed craven and sad.

I jumped in. "During the week he is mustering up his nerve, his own company could get wind that he has been interviewing and fire him on the spot. Now he has lost leverage to negotiate his offer higher, and his benefits won't pick up on the new job for ninety days: one health crisis away from potential financial ruin. Or he might get calls from companies he sent résumés to a month ago asking him to interview. Should he? Does he ask for more time? Maybe his wife has gotten used to their schedule the way it is, and she starts working on him to stay where he is and not take the risk. Meantime Harper here is calling every day. Don't deny it, Harper, you've done it to me!"

"I not only don't deny it, I take pride in it. It is my duty as the client's agent to get an answer. And that brings us to another life variable: me. Say you don't accept the job right away and I assume you are going to say no. That means I start sending other candidates in right now to protect the client and myself. Sometimes they're strong candidates, they cost less, or they're prepared to accept the job right away. And the client is tired of waiting for you."

Had Harper sent other candidates to Wallace? He wouldn't do that to me, would he? Unemployment, like loneliness, makes you paranoid.

"And it is not always that Machiavellian," he said. "Sometimes during your decision making, companies lose budget monies and impose hiring freezes. Most offers are accepted within forty-eight hours in successful deals in my firm."

I thought about the offers I had received over the years, and Harper was right. The jobs I took, I took immediately or within a day.

"Can you remember when Mark first told you he loved you, Leena?"

"Of course."

"How long before you responded?"

"Immediately. I felt the same way."

"But if you had told him you needed a week or so to consider your options and that you were confident, given your feelings, you probably would come back to him with an affirmation, how do you think that would have gone over?"

"I think I'd still be trying to write pithy wall postings on Facebook to every cute guy I knew."

"Right. So here's what we know: a company has interviewed a series of people and then selected you. They not only want you, but they want you to feel the same way about them. Every day you think about it, their feelings for you are diminished. Accept in a day and the emotion is matched and a career is launched. Accept in a week and they can't help but feel you took the job because your preferred options didn't work out. You 'ended up' with them.

"Offers are how companies say 'I love you,' and they need to hear it back. Have either of you ever said 'I love you' and not heard it back?"

"Yes," Leena said. "It was horrible."

"Me, too. And it sucked."

"Really? That was rhetorical. It's never happened to me. What is wrong with you two?"

My Blackberry buzzed, and the familiar red light started flashing—a text from Peter: "Are you going to be much longer? I have another client soon."

Is he joking? He is aware and respectful of his client's time but couldn't text, call, or email in three days?

Harper continued:

HARPER'S RULES
Time Kills Deals, Part Three

There is no such thing as 'I don't have time' in the modern world. Technology has stripped away many of the classic excuses, so when people cling stubbornly to them, they can cause frustration and even hostile action that both parties come to regret.

If you are like most people, you probably check your email twenty to twenty-five times a day. And you probably either read or write email or instant messages up to three hours of your day. And it's likely that at some point you've had a Blackberry or some other smart-phone to stay connected to the office or clients. And you obviously have voice mail, which you check after seeing the indicator light go on. How soon do you check your voice mail after seeing you have one?

"Five minutes? What if a client wanted to schedule an interview or something was wrong with Madison? That's my son, Casey."

Okay, everyone I know is having babies, and everyone is naming them after presidents. If I hear of one named Grover or Millard, I may renounce my citizenship.

The truth is, technology was supposed to free us up so that we would not have to be chained to the office in order to receive information. Instead we are imprisoned by it. We are petrified of missing anything. We are never not working.

For the first time in history, when asked, 'If you left your wallet and your cell phone at home, which would you go back for, if either?' the majority of people polled say they would only go back for the cell. We will go without money or proof of identity, but we won't go without our real sense of identity, our connection to the world.

Technology exposes the truth about time-killing deals. We can't say we don't have time, we can't say we didn't get that message, we can't say we're not in a place where we can respond. If we say those things, we are only delaying, and a delay is usually a 'no' on a deferment plan.

"So, Harper, you have been ducking me about Wallace Avery? You have bad news, and you haven't had the moxie to call and let me know. Right?"

Harper exhaled deeply. His voice seemed milky and distant.

It seemed I was about to lose my opportunity with InterAnnex, the only viable return to employment I had, and all I could feel was alarm at how tired and dazed Harper suddenly sounded.

"Nothing has been decided, so let's dial down the drama," he began. "But yes, some concerns have surfaced."

"I don't get it. What could surface?"

"He checked references, okay? Normal due diligence."

"Of course he did; I provided them. My references rock."

"One that you didn't provide apparently did not."

"Who?"

"I don't know. Casey, this happens. I will deal with it."

"How are you dealing with it, Harper? By sending in other candidates?"

I had gone too far; Leena felt she had to come to his defense.

"We haven't sent in even one other résumé, Ms. Matthews," she said.

"You don't know what it's like, neither one of you. You don't know what it's like to be alone and have everything unravel."

Harper laughed softly: a sad laugh—tired.

"I have to go, Casey," he said, and for a moment I thought his voice would crack. "I will get to the bottom of this, and we'll talk soon about the realities of reference checking."

"Okay. I thought everyone loved me. You'd think, given all the evidence to the contrary, I would know better." I could see Peter handing a towel and a plastic bottle of water to his client as a reward for her set of squats.

"Leena, can you give us a minute, please?"

"Sure. I'll speak to you soon. Hang in there."

I waited until I could assume she was gone. "Harper, I struggle daily with the question of just how good a person I am, but I am an excellent salesperson. I really am, and I just . . . I need you to know that. I don't care what someone said about me. I do care what you think about me."

"Casey, I love you to death, but if you weren't excellent at what you do, if I couldn't place you and make money off you, I wouldn't waste a moment of my time with you."

This outright lie made me laugh, which made him think I believed him, which made him happy.

"Are you okay, Harper? Give me credit for not asking until Leena was gone."

"I am perfection personified. Bye, Casey."

Who told Wallace something negative about me? An ex-boss? A colleague? It was so frustrating being judged without being able to defend myself.

I just wanted to go home. But as I retrieved my car keys from the rack, Peter yelled my name from down the hall. I could have kept going; I didn't.

"Were you just going to leave without even talking to me?"

"Yes."

"But I have a whole speech."

"Peter, look . . . no."

"Let me give you the Twitter version then, 140 characters or less."

"Go. I'm counting."

"I didn't call you because I didn't know if I should. Did you hear anything about me? Something bad?"

I nodded slowly. I owed him.

He smiled the way actors do at the Oscars at the precise moment it is announced they did not win, and yet the whole world is watching to see how gracefully they handle the pain.

"It's not fair, you know. People talk, but not to your face. I would have told you; it just didn't seem cool on the first date. As much as everyone talks about moving on, no one really lets you do it."

Had I judged Peter on a bad reference?

"Okay, you went over. But it was pretty good. I'd like to see you again."

Before he could hug or kiss me, I turned and actually sauntered out.

Harper made me join Facebook. I told him I didn't want to, that I was in touch with everyone I wanted to be in touch with, but he called me on it. Harper is the only man who calls me on things, at least the only man whom I continue to talk to after he calls me on things.

"By not joining, you are making a statement: You are too good for us."

"Okay, I'll join. But I'm putting a picture of Starbucks up on my main profile. And I'm not tagging photos and relentlessly informing friends of my most trivial daily events."

"As an unemployed person, it is irresponsible of you not to post your status and subtly request help."

And as I logged in, sure enough, I had a response to my status ("Casey is crazy busy interviewing, still looking for that perfect-fit senior sales role for a technology company").

It was from my old boss, Mike Ogilvy. He said hi, that he didn't know I was looking, and that he would ask around.

So Mike is off my list of suspects for whoever sabotaged my reference with Wallace Avery. I used the Find Friends function and, after taking a couple calming breaths, typed "Tyrus Conway."

Ty must be in his early sixties now. Facebook has truly become ubiquitous if Ty comes up. Seven years ago, he was part of the company's mentoring program: twice a month a senior rep would travel with a junior rep to offer critiques and shore up any product knowledge or salesmanship issues. Ty called me "honey," which I chalked up to a generational divide. But by the second meeting I had concerns: a hand on my backside guiding me through revolving doors; leaning in and whispering to me in a crowded elevator.

But the red flag vibe came after a couple of drinks while stranded at O'Hare. The ruddy face, the expansive mood, and the wide-open pores were obvious evidence that he had a drinking problem. Two hours later, when we got to the hotel, checked in, and walked to the elevators, he asked me what room I was in. I hesitated. His eyes narrowed and he dramatically put down his bags.

"Listen, young lady, you and I have to work together. I suppose you think every man in the world is trying to make a move on you. But I am fifty-six, married for thirty-four years to the mother of my children. No offense, you ain't worth losing her over. I asked which room you were in so that when our customer calls in the morning to schedule the demo, I could buzz your room. But just call me when you wake up."

I apologized and gave him my room number. But as soon as I had gotten settled in—and had called Donald to say good night and to have him put Starbuck's head close to the receiver's mouthpiece so that I could hear her purring—I had a tap at the door. I opened the door two inches and could smell the bourbon on Ty's breath.

I began my "go sleep it off" speech, but I didn't get four words in before he pushed open the door, grabbed me around my waist, pinned me against the wall, and began kissing my neck and face.

It's a blur now, but I remember, in no particular order, a simultaneous gouging of his face and kneeing of his groin. I remember screaming, and because the door was still open, it was just a few seconds before a kid named Ron, delivering room service two rooms down, had Ty pinned on the ground. By midnight the CEO was reassuring me that this would be dealt with through both legal and corporate channels. I only bristled once when he told me he was sure I had nothing to do with provoking the behavior. "You're damn right I didn't," I said. "I got served up to this joker, and I have rights, too!"

Ty never came back to work. I knew he was suspended, but I don't know if he eventually quit to spare himself the ignominy or if they fired him. Ty was not a bad person, just weak and ruined.

Was Ty Conway sabotaging my reference with Wallace?

Can anyone just say whatever they want about someone and because it's a "reference check" get away with it? Aren't there laws?

My answer came to me in the form of Facebook's instant messaging. I can't even bust Harper about being on Facebook when he should be working; networking *is* working for him. I told him I was confused about the ethics and legalities of reference checks. He responded that I should check my email. Apparently I had inspired another chapter for his book.

HARPER'S RULES
Reference Checks—What Are Your Rights?

On one end of the spectrum, one can check a reference and the report is absurdly positive: the subject walked on water; was not only the best worker/employee ever, but as a human being should have been canonized at the end of her first fiscal year. On the other end, if the reference is negative, it can be searing: the person was ineffective, inefficient, incompetent, and, from a personal perspective, whether the person was the Antichrist was openly and seriously discussed.

But is any of it true? What is the vested interest of the party making the statement? What bridge was burned, what transgression unforgiven? These questions are critical for a simple reason: hiring decisions are often made based on reference checks. And where is that grey line of slander or defamation? When does opinion become actionable? And how do we (companies, recruiters, candidates) protect ourselves?

Luckily for us, there are rules, rights, and laws.

The Fair Credit Reporting Act, (enacted in 1971 and amended in 1996 and 1998), governs the reference checking done by recruiting/search firms on behalf of specific and prospective employers. The purpose of the law is to ensure that those charged with the responsibility of checking references exercise this duty gravely: "with fairness, impartiality, and respect for the right to privacy." There are real teeth to this legislation. Willful failure creates a liability for the recruiter that could result in punitive damages. These damages, and associated court and attorney fees, will always be far greater than the fee the recruiter could earn by violating the law. No quality recruiter would take such a risk.

Your rights as a candidate:

1. Your recruiter must get your permission to check any reference.
2. Your recruiter must, upon request, accurately disclose the nature and substance of the information, but the source need not be disclosed.
   (So you get to know what was said about you, but not who said it. This drives candidates crazy, but it allows for more candor and less fear of reprisal.)
3. You have the right to receive the reference content in writing within five business days.
4. The recruiting firm must keep these records for two years.
5. Some info, if obtained through a third-party reference-checking firm, may not be disclosed: e.g., bankruptcies if over fourteen years old, paid tax liens, and arrest records, if over seven years old.

I still didn't get it. I can find out what was said about me but not who said it? If I don't know who is trashing me, how do I know whom to confront, or failing that, whom to leave off my damn list of references? And if the recruiter can only call the references I provide, how did Wallace get a bad reference Harper doesn't know about? I was about to call Harper to get to the bottom of all of this when I saw he had provided an FAQ section.

REFERENCE CHECK FAQS

Q: Do companies really put any stock in references? Aren't they loaded? I am only going to give references I'm sure will say great things.

A: Novice headhunters are always shocked when they learn that more than seventy percent of the time, the reference tells the truth, even if it could hurt a candidate's chance of getting a job. This is as it should be. These references are bosses and hiring authorities themselves, and they take telling the truth on a reference as a matter of duty and honor.

Q: Does that mean my boss lied when he said he'd give a positive reference?

A: Absolutely not! It means an experienced headhunter or HR professional asked penetrating and difficult questions. Keep in mind many references are done at the end of the interviewing process when you have had several meetings and people have started to form opinions about you. So when your ex-boss is asked, "Does he have a temper issue when his authority is challenged?" and that is a matter of record in your work experience, he feels obliged to discuss it.

Q: I am going on a final interview, and I'm pretty sure they're going to make me an offer. I have 101 credits toward my bachelor's degree, but I never finished due to some family stuff I will spare you. But I went four years and did all the classes my major required and . . . well, here's the deal. On my résumé it says I have a BA degree. Will they check? Can they?

A: They can and usually do, and if you get caught, they will not hire you. Colleges and universities keep the strictest of records. (Their legal accreditation depends on it.)

Q: Do you have to have perfect references to get hired? I was immature at my first couple of jobs and made some bad choices. Is it going to follow me forever?

A: Here is what I tell all my candidates. *Find* me a bad reference. That's right! Because if you don't, the company will take your three "perfect" references and discount them. Here is what you must understand: companies are made up of humans making decisions. And these humans are flawed. They don't trust or believe references without negatives. Give me three excellent references and one "bad" (as long as the bad part is not morally reprehensible or occupationally egregious; I can't place a murderer just released from prison or an embezzler in a CFO's job) and companies will hire you. Give me just the three excellent references, and they feel they are not getting the whole story.

I remembered when Donald said it was time, about four months into our relationship, to become exclusive. I asked why, and he said, "You're perfect to me, Casey. I can't find anything about you I don't like." And the moment was horrible, because I lost respect for his judgment. Give me one negative; maybe then I'll believe you really love me.

The last FAQ could have been written about me and helped me see why Harper could not prevent, and did not cause, Wallace Avery's concern about me.

Q: I was told by someone on the inside at the company that I didn't get the job because of a bad reference, but my recruiter swears he submitted the rave references that I supplied him. What gives?

A: Your question has been the bane of my existence. The Fair Credit Reporting Act applies to third-party firms like me and your recruiter. The companies themselves are free to "network" and check with people they know who know you. Because you want the job and your recruiter makes money if you get the job, companies tend to believe the "networked reference" more than they do you or your recruiter. It is a flaw in the law, but it is also human nature.

So that's it. Wallace went beyond Harper, asked around about me, and found something. Now Harper is trying to backtrack for me.

I am a divorced woman who was publicly humiliated, and I still don't consider Donald an enemy. I think Donald is a really good guy who acted like a total idiot for too long. He openly cheated on me and ignored sacred vows, but I still think of him as the most decent and trustworthy guy I ever knew.

Just before I logged out, I saw that Facebook had listed Abby Taylor as a "friend suggestion." I always adored Abby, but she was one of the spoils of divorce; Donald got Abby. On a whim, I sent Abby an invite anyway. Starbucks distracted me for a second, and by the time I looked back on the screen Abby had already accepted me. I went to her page, looked at her photo, and saw her most recent status update: "Shopping for my friend Sasha's baby shower. Don't tell Joe, but it makes me want another baby. Someone slap me silly."

Donald wanted kids from day one and I held him off. Of course they were going to get pregnant. At some level I knew this would happen.

So why am I upset? I grabbed my cell phone and scrolled to Donald's number. It irritated me to no end that he was still "scrollable." I didn't know how to defriend someone on Facebook. Maybe there *was* no bad reference; maybe Wallace was just appalled that a young woman with a relatively high disposable income had no children. Maybe he just didn't want someone so self-absorbed on his sales team.

My cell phone vibrated. Harper. Thank God.

"Harper, I'm going to be thirty-five in three weeks. A lot of people die at seventy. I could be halfway through my life, I am middle-aged, and what have I got? I'll tell you what . . . Nothing!"

"I'm going to go out on a limb and guess that I caught you at a bad time. Casey, I got the name. Doria Colangelo."

My depression was instantly swept away in a cleansing rush of anger.

"Doria Colangelo. My God."

"According to the story she has told people that know Wallace, when you worked together at ParaSource, you knowingly sold an untested home health-care solution to a hospital alliance. She claims your error forced ParaSource to do a second rollout for free in order to avoid a lawsuit. She said you buried key data to close the deal. She's made it seem pretty ugly."

"That's what she said, huh?"

"Look, I know it's not true. I know there's the official and the unofficial version. Tell me what happened, I pass your version on to Wallace, he gives you the benefit of the doubt, and we get past this. Wallace likes you. So tell me."

Doria cut corners. She would show up late for software training sessions and as a result would routinely tell customers our product could do something it couldn't, forcing someone to do damage control. And she was a user; someone was always cutting and pasting a PowerPoint for her because she got home so late the night before that she had "ran out of runway." Somehow this was overlooked by management, and it infuriated the sales staff, especially the women who were older and not as willing to wear skirts way above the knee or shirts unbuttoned practically to the navel.

The *coup de grâce* came after Doria finished her second full quarter dead last among our sales team and was inexplicably added to the coveted health-care vertical. I was promoted to health care because I had been 140 percent of my goal for the year. I was thrilled because health care is where the money is in the twenty-first century. Every software company in its right mind was peddling software solutions to hospitals, clinics, and universities. And our technologists came up with an awesome one—a "have to have." In software sales, you want to be a "have to have", not a "nice to have."

"Nice to have" software is the home abdominal machine you ordered at 2 A.M. after inhaling a box of Oreos.

A "have to have" means your business couldn't run without it, or it saves you so much money you must buy it. Windows, Word, Quicken, Excel . . . the giants of the "have to haves." Every salesperson wants to sell the "have to haves," and we are no different in our dating lives. When I think of my marriage, Donald was my "nice to have," and I was his "have to have." Until I was not.

Our tech guys came up with a killer "have to have" app for our home health-care vertical. We all knew this product would rock. And then, one of our developers came up with the icing on the cake for the app: voice recognition. With this, we would completely bury the competition. We would be bulletproof.

Our tech team made it very clear that the product was ready for rollout and implementation, but that it would take six months to a year to have voice recognition fully functional.

Doria's casual relationship with the truth either didn't allow her to hear this part, or she chose to ignore it. A couple of months later, she called me and asked if I wanted to split a deal. She had a hospital alliance in Brattleboro very close to committing to a three-year, three-million-dollar deal on the new application, but she had to get past a final presentation to the chief technologists and the CFO. This was known to be my specialty. Doria said she would give me one third of the commission dollars if I went on the final meeting with her. This is found money, and as much as I was reluctant to partner up with someone known to be sloppy, mercurial, and untested, it made no financial sense not to do it.

I could tell the CFO loved Doria and wanted to make this happen. It could potentially save them a ton of money, so why not? Win-win, right?

And then the CFO made a request.

"And Doria, we decided we want the voice recognition built in, so you can implement that as well, right?"

I looked at Doria, but she kept her eyes focused on the CFO and, like all good liars, was not at all thrown.

"No worries. I'll take care of it."

Anticipating my ire, on the way home she told me she would call back and explain the voice recognition would be implemented as soon as it was available, but that it would not come with the package.

"You better spell that out, sister, and document it so they don't call you on it later."

And that was the end of it. It wasn't my deal.

Then my boss called me while I was on the road in D.C. saying he wanted to talk to me when I got back later in the week about the Brattleboro deal. He wouldn't elaborate. An hour later I got a call from Doria saying she needed to talk and would I have lunch with her? I said I was in D.C. and she said she knew I was, that I was at the Fairmont and she was in the lobby.

At lunch, Doria told me she was a mess and needed someone to talk to. Her brother, Austin, her mentor and hero, the person she loved the most in the world, was very sick. He had already had kidney cancer when he was a teenager, but they removed the kidney before it had spread. Now, a decade later, it was back. If he didn't receive a transplanted kidney quickly, he would be gone. She told me all this in fragments because she kept having to stop to cry and gather herself.

The doctors recommended everyone in the family be evaluated as possible donors. She said "of course," made the appointment, and pulled a no-show. She loved her brother more than anyone she had ever known. And yet she didn't want to give him her kidney. She didn't want to get cut into, she didn't want to be sick, she didn't want to live in fear of losing her one remaining kidney.

This was such an extraordinary display of vulnerability and honesty I was blown away. To have the courage to admit something so monstrously selfish showed a depth to Doria I didn't know existed. We held hands. We cried. We were a mess, make-up ruined, and when she asked if she could come to my room to freshen up, I didn't think anything of it. When we got to the room, she noticed my laptop and asked if she could log in to work and check on some things. I told her I was already connected and just to close me out and help herself. When I came out of the bedroom ready to go to my client, she closed the laptop quickly. Her mood had improved tremendously. Suddenly she was in a hurry.

Later that week I came in to meet my boss, T. J., a former top producer who had crossed over to management. I stopped at my desk, and there was a gift-wrapped bottle of Dom Perignon and a card from Doria. She wanted me to know the doctors had found a donor for Austin.

As soon as I sat down opposite T. J., he told me he wanted me to know he was disappointed in me, that I wasn't as clever as I thought.

I assured him I had no idea in hell what he was talking about.

"Casey, our profit on the Brattleboro rollout would be around 300K after taxes. But because you promised them a voice-recognition component we cannot currently provide, they want to cancel the implementation, and if we claim breach of contract, they will sue for—guess what?—about 300K."

"I never promised them any such thing. I was not the account manager who wrote up that deal and you know it. I made a cameo appearance to close the thing for a rookie."

He removed a document from a folder and placed it in front of me. It was a printout of an email from me to Doria. I looked at the time and date. I had to smile. Doria had sent it from my account in my hotel room at the Fairmont, written by her on my laptop. She wrote on my behalf that we had to find a way to get Geoff to okay the voice-recognition beta for Brattleboro, or find some way to buy time on the implementation, or the whole thing "was going to blow up in our faces."

I felt pure hate, a liquid current coursing through me. I calmly handed the document to my boss and told him I never wrote it.

"Who did?" he asked. I lifted my head and stared directly into his eyes.

"Did Doria have access to your email?"

I nodded.

"Can you prove it?"

"No, and I won't try. You know me, you know her. Make the call."

"What did you to do to her that would make her go this far?"

"Nothing. That's the beauty of it. In a way, I think she likes me a lot."

He exhaled deeply and sat back in his chair.

"I don't know why I gave up selling for management. You people exhaust me."

I got an email the next day saying management was "satisfied the misunderstanding was not of my making, and no permanent record would be in my file, nor action taken." Doria was gone within a month. I never thought I'd hear her name again.

"So," Harper said, "you've taken your Samuel Beckett pause to gather yourself. Now give me your side of the story so I can fight this with Wallace."

"You can tell Wallace it's not true. But that's all you can tell him."

"Casey, that won't be good enough."

"Where does it end, Harper? You can call it reference checking, and granted, employers need to know whom they are hiring. But I don't care what the law says, the system is flawed; it doesn't get at the truth. The truth is somewhere in the middle; that's where it lives. If that costs me the job, so be it. Bye, Harper."

It wasn't until after I hung up and started unloading my dishwasher that I realized I had plagiarized from Donald and what he said to me the day we passed the point of no return.

"Do you want to be with her?" I had asked.

"Yes."

"Then you don't love me."

"I do. The truth is in the middle; that's where it lives."

I dried my hands and reached for my phone. I knew he would recognize my number.
"Casey?"

"So I'm thinking Casey works as a girl's name or a boy's name, just in case you get a girl but want a boy and decide to use her name as a way to scar her for life."

"I was going to tell you," Donald said.

"No, you weren't."

"No, I wasn't. But I'm glad you know now."

"I'm really happy for you, Donny. You'll be a spectacular dad."

"God," he sighed, "I hope so."

"Remember the macaroni and cheese?" I said.

He had set the table with our best linens and our formal dishes; wine awaited me at the door. A sex setup normally, but Donald's plan was to formally ask me to begin trying to have a baby. He said it was time, that in order for love to be sustained, it had to be immersed in growth. It didn't work; I talked him off the ledge. Resigned, he brought out the macaroni and cheese.

"It was lame," I said. "I want you to know, if you had made better macaroni and cheese that night, we might have a five-year-old now. Live with that, Donald."

Donald cracked up. I knew that no one, not Sasha or, God forbid, anyone that comes after her, could make him laugh like I could.

"So, now that it doesn't matter, why didn't you want to have a family with me? Did you know we weren't going to make it even then?" he said.

A fair question, and since I called him, I guess I owed it to him to tell the truth, even though it remains in the middle.

"No, Donny, it was me. All I could think of then was what children would cost me. How would I be able to still be the top producer in the company? I didn't think I could handle the costs."

"I understand," he said.

"No, listen. What I wish someone had told me is that when they are your kids, you don't want to do the things you used to do. I'm so sorry I made you wait, Donny."

"When did you figure this out?" he asked.

"I can pinpoint the moment. When Sheila woke up and wouldn't eat breakfast until we went out and got the mail. We started walking up the driveway, and she reached out and took my hand. And the way her tiny little hand felt, it was only a hundred feet to the mailbox, I don't know, it just hit me. There was no way the day was going to get any better than this."

Donald politely waited until I had stopped crying, told me he had to go, and said he was glad that I had called.

"And Casey," he added, "it's not too late for you. Whenever you are ready, you will be an incredible mother."

How about that? After all that's happened, Donald is still willing to be my reference.

My cell buzzed; it was Harper. I was feeling so cleansed by my confession to Donald that even Harper couldn't ruin my mood.

"Harper, before you start in on me—you have never been divorced or unemployed. So you don't know how liberating it can feel, how nice it can be to not be a part of anything. It's a shame you will never know this simple and sweet feeling. I feel sort of sorry for you."

There was a dead pause. I thought we had lost the signal.

"I called Wallace Avery and told him exactly what you told me to tell him," he said, finally. "Now it's my turn, young lady. I need to know from here on out that you are going to do exactly what I tell you to do until you are drawing a paycheck."

"You are such a buzz-kill, Harper. Deal. Was Avery furious?"

"Oh yeah, but not at you. Turns out your old boss T. J. and Wallace are tight. So Wallace is furious at Doria and at me, for not knowing the story. You he loves. The blind loyalty, the principled stand, the rising above the mean-spiritedness—he was impressed."

"What about you, Harper? Were you impressed?"

"I thought you were being foolish and stubborn. Anyway, game on with InterAnnex. Wallace wants to set up a final interview, but he needs a couple of weeks so he can get to the Pacific Rim and set up some supply channels. That gives us a chance to send you out on more interviews."

"Harper, if Wallace wants to hire me, I don't want . . . okay, right, whatever you say. I'm in, boss."

"Good. And . . . I am aware of what feeling liberated is like."

Was he finally going to talk to me? Earlier the day before, when I told myself I would check Indeed.com for job postings, I went to Harper's website and found pics in the "About Us" section: the principals and their wives dancing, a group photo of all the attendees. Harper stood alone in every picture.

"You know when I feel liberated?" he said. "You land at the airport after a business trip. You take the valet shuttle to your car, and that's the moment. It is thrilling to be back in your car. You realize you love your car, and even though you are just minutes away from having been in a plane going 600 mph, it is now that you feel fast and loose and free.

"But it doesn't last long. And before you know it, you're home, and the feeling's gone." His voice was distant, muted, and sad.

CHAPTER TEN

OTHER OFFERS
AND PLAYING THE FIELD

I knew I was supposed to keep expenses down to the absolute essentials, but I decided my massage therapist qualified.

"So how are things, chica?" Lucy asked. "Same old same old?"

"Things are good," I said, and it surprised me to realize that I wasn't lying. I have always had a built-in survival mechanism. I expect the worst possible outcome. Always. So when I get a punch to the solar plexus from life, it not only doesn't throw me, but I can legitimately say to myself, "Is that the worst of it? Is that all you got? That's not so bad."

And as Lucy did her magic, I took stock. My final interview with InterAnnex was back on; I still had a couple of months of severance; and since our showdown at the gym, Peter and I had gone out twice, and it was great. The second date was a totally safe daytripper. I went to his softball league playoff game and played the role of cool chick. I wore their team cap on backward, cheered loudly, and when a foul ball came into the stands, I caught it and threw it back to the umpire with confidence and skill. A couple of nights later, trying to show some range, Peter took me to a lecture series about the changing technological world order by *New York Times* guru Thomas Friedman. Peter was lost, but I so appreciated the sweet gesture. He had clients at 5 A.M. the next morning, so we brought separate cars, and other than a very well executed good night kiss, it was a pretty old-fashioned date. We both knew our next date meant we were about to cross over into intimacy. I couldn't wait.

In the waiting room was my entrepreneurial hero, Sophie Dunham, the owner of Drive-by Pet Sitting. She was a one-woman show. For fourteen dollars she would come to your house, feed your cat or dog, walk them or change a litter box, play with them with a wide variety of cool toys she brought with her, and leave you a report card evaluating the visit. She graded them for things like "fuzziness," "quality of tail thumping," and "enthusiasm for yarn." Sophie knew intuitively that people like me considered our pets our kids, and I often would sit Starbucks down when Donald and I would return from a weekend away and say gravely, "You couldn't have been a little fuzzier?" Sophie's husband had been transferred to Topeka, and although she made a very good living with Drive-by Pet Sitting, she could do it anywhere.

"Know anybody who wants to buy my business?" she said when I saw her. "Flex hours, you play with pets all day, and last year I made 125K."

I told Sophie I would think about it, gave her a hug and wished her well on her move to what she referred to as "godforsaken Topeka," and by the time I got to my car, I already envisioned my new life. I have always preferred animals to people; I prefer their company, their attitude, and their worldview. They are happy unless given a reason to feel bad. People are just the opposite.

Even I could live on 125K if I wasn't buying clothes and competing in the world of enterprise sales. This was my chance to take my life in a totally different direction! Where was it written that I had to stay on the same path? I was scrolling for Sophie's number in my Blackberry when I noticed two voice mails, Harper and an unknown number.

"Harper," I began, with no pretense of a greeting, "I'm sorry to do this to you, but I owe it to you to be totally upfront. I have decided to go into business for myself."

"No you haven't," he said, sounding almost bored.

"I haven't?"

"Three words. Bed and breakfast."

Damn. The last time Harper placed me I called him from a bed and breakfast in New Hampshire. I was on the wraparound front porch looking at an incredible view of the White Mountains. It was autumn, peak colors, I saw the FOR SALE sign, and called Harper to tell him I was buying the place.

"You don't want to own a bed and breakfast," he said. "You want to live in one."

He was right, and I knew it.

"So why did you call, Harper? I mean, besides to quash my dreams?"

"I have two other companies that need a senior sales rep in the Northeast, and they both want to talk to you. I'm having Leena send you the job descriptions. We'll get you in front of both of them before you go back to meet Wallace."

"I have to return another call, Harper." And I hung up. Quash my dreams, deal a deathblow to Park and Bark or whatever, and feel my wrath. I did have the unknown voice mail—at least I wasn't lying.

The voice wasn't familiar. He spoke quickly in the practiced, high-intensity inflection of the professional salesperson.

"Hi, Casey, it's Jamie Post. I have no idea if you remember me or our conversation. Anyway I don't want to get into this in voice mail; I will send you an email. But I'll take the mystery out of this for you. Bottom line, the word is out that you are available, and I wanted to talk to you about that. So call me or respond to my email. Thanks. Hope you're well. Jamie Post—555-334-4309."

Jamie Post? I'm great with faces, but names—not so much. I had to assume this was Harper's viral marketing paying off. I had put my obligatory posting on Facebook, done a mass email blast to all my contacts on LinkedIn, and had left a message or sent résumés to every VP of sales I knew or almost knew, using the scripted verbiage Harper had supplied. Guess this guy Post has something for me. I was about to Google him before I returned his call, but his promised email showed up in my Blackberry just as I was logging into my browser. At least he followed up. I respect that in any salesperson.

TO: CMatthews@Yahoo.com
FROM: JDPOST@Dresserindustries.com
SUBJECT: Remains to be seen!
Hi Casey,

I just left you a voice mail. You are young, and the young answer their email and text long before they check their voice mails. My daughter (don't pretend you recall), a 15-year-old force of nature, tells me to stop wasting my time leaving her voice mails. If I want to talk to her, text her. ("Really, Dad, dial in, enter a code, listen to a playback? Life is too short for voice mail.") So . . . okay, there is no segue that is not impossibly awkward here. I am the guy who you chatted with five years ago on the train from Norwalk to Grand Central. I hear through the grapevine, (There I go dating myself. I'm supposed to say "network." Well give me credit, I just stopped saying "rolodex.") that you are divorced. I was when we chatted and still am. I wondered if you'd consider having dinner with me this week sometime. Pick a day, I am all too available.

Warm Regards,
Jamie

PS . . . The guy on the train with the chalk-stripe suit and the umbrella trying desperately to get your attention away from the *Times*. Damn Maureen Dowd.

Jamie Post! I had a married woman's crush on him; I knew our relationship would end when the doors of the train opened at Grand Central. He was late thirties to early forties then, but already lots of silver in the thick wavy hair he would clearly never lose.

His eyes kept darting over to me, waiting for me to put the paper down and give him a way in.

"Maureen Dowd, right?" he said after I chuckled out loud. "The piece on Bush channeling Brad Pitt in *Troy*?"

I nodded.

"She's cheerful, yet vicious. Kind of hot, too."

"I'm pretty sure she's single."

"She'd eat me alive."

"Not many men would admit that."

"Oh, I still have illusions. Maureen Dowd just isn't one of them. Actually that piece kind of made me sad. It's about our obsession with celebrity, right? When I was a little kid, Elvis died, and my dad cried. When I was a teenager John Lennon goes down, and my older brother flipped out. When my turn came with Kurt Cobain, I didn't feel anything but that he had made a stupid choice."

Okay, maybe this was his standard procedure for hitting on women in trains, but if it was, it worked. I was caught up.

"Don't you think that's a good thing," I asked, "that you care more about the people who are actually in your life?"

"I'm not sure. It makes me wonder if I'm just too hollow. You look like you're my ex-wife's age—"

Adroit. A nice touch . . .

"—Crying jags over Princess Diana? Calling in sick so you could watch the funeral?"

"No, I'm more like you. I felt terrible for the children, but to me the saddest thing was giving Elton John an excuse to plug another name into 'Goodbye Norma Jean.'"

"We could form a club!" he said when he stopped laughing. "We'll meet every time a celebrity dies and toast to the unknown loved ones we care nothing about."

"Sorry," I said. "No can do."

"Because of that ring on your finger?"

"Well that, and I don't qualify. JFK, Jr.? I was a basket case. He and I were going to end up together."

He laughed again, and his eyes made me wish Grand Central were farther away. "I'm Jamie Post, by the way."

An hour after I got Jamie's messages, I was sharing a smoothie with Hannah at the juice bar of the health food store less than two blocks from the gym. Even being this close to Peter and discussing another man made me feel awful, but since I called the emergency meeting, I had to let Hannah pick the place. She *had* to have a smoothie.

"So," she began, "Jamie Post would fall into Category One."

"He would?"

"The ones that got away. You regret it, you romanticize them out of proportion to what they were, you look them up online and stalk from afar. It's why I'm on Facebook. Go out with the guy."

"Hannah, I am dating Peter."

"A couple of times! There's been no sex."

"Sex is looming."

"Now you sound like Ben, then I come back from brushing my teeth and you're snoring."

"You're saying I go out with Jamie?"

"How can you not? You talked about that damn train ride for months."

"I did? I guess I did. What about Peter?"

"How do you know he's not seeing other people?"

"He would tell me."

Hannah rolled her eyes. "Okay, then tell him the truth. This guy resurfaced, you have feelings, you need to play this out, you don't have a commitment with Peter, you are being upfront and you hope he can appreciate it."

"Is that what you would do?"

"Honey, I would have slept with him on the train."

As I walked to my car the reality set in. If I really cared about Peter, I wouldn't want to see another man. Peter adores me. I don't really know Jamie. He is older than me, has a teenager, has been divorced a long time—there has to be a story behind that, right? I wondered all this aloud to Hannah before she took her last, annoying loud suck on her smoothie.

"Duh. Because he reminds you of Harper."

I tried to imagine Peter calling me and telling me some random girl from back in the day had reached out to him and since we were not yet "committed," he was going to see her and wanted to be upfront. I would be devastated. If I had any arts and crafts skills I would make a voodoo doll and spend the appointed evening poking it in the groin with a pin.

And yet, I was about to seriously consider thinking about planning on calling Jamie . . .

Suddenly I was in my driveway. I didn't remember taking my exit or making the turn on Boynton or crossing Chevas, but here I am. I started my day with a relaxing massage, and now my chest feels tight and my shoulders ache. I carry no house key because I have a garage door opener and never go in through the front door. I sat zoned out for a full minute before I realized the door had only raised two feet off the ground.

I hit the remote about twelve times before giving up and going to the front entrance, lifting the welcome mat, and picking up my key. "You can't hide it in a planter or buy one of those fake rocks that hold keys?" my mother asks. No, I can't. It ruins the irony of a burglar getting access to everything I own by lifting a mat that promises WEL-COME. I can live without valuables, but not without irony.

Before I could even get inside, I heard a man yell my name and come trotting across my yard. He was tall and rugged looking, the deep leathery tan of a guy who works outside for a living. He flashed a big smile and shook my hand. He informed me he was from the housing development association. He was sorry, this was the part of the job he hated, but there had been complaints from the neighbors about my lawn. He handed me a document, which he said was a "warning." He assured me it was just a formality.

"You're telling me that people complained because my lawn wasn't mowed?"

"Like I said, no worries. We get it mowed, we tear that up, it goes away."

"I just don't get it. Don't they have lives? I am *busy*. I live alone, I travel for a living."

"Oh, well, that makes it tough. Where do you work?"

"That is not relevant!" I said, in the Laura Linney–district attorney manner I adopt when I am embarrassed.

My cell going off saved him further ire he didn't deserve. It was Lucy. Did I forget to pay her for the massage? No, I remember leaving the cash under the little Buddha statue.

"Hey. Apollo was in here today. He just left."

Apollo is Steve Adamzyk, a male model, incredibly beautiful, and he is not gay. Lucy gets to manhandle him once a month and get paid for it.

"He asked for your number."

"What? What is going on here? Who opened this spigot? Did I unknowingly change perfume?"

"You smell great," Lawn Man said.

I waved my finger at him.

"Can I give him your number?" Lucy asked.

"I don't even know him. I see him in your lobby once in a while."

"You don't have to know him. Do I need to remind you that I see him naked, front and back? There is *ample* reason for you to take his call. So give him your number, right?"

"No. Yes . . . I need to think about it. I have to go. Wait, does he mow lawns?"

I hung up and looked out at my lawn. It looked like hell. Everything felt like it was slipping again, and Lawn Man could sense I was about to lose it in front of him.

"Listen, once a week I do the Randall's yard down the street," he said. "I could swing by and do your place in no time. No charge. Okay?"

"The Randalls are, like, 300 years old. Each. They can't do their own lawn. I can."

"You travel for a living; you're not around."

"I'm not working right now. I lied about that. I just suck."

"I do the Randall's day after tomorrow; I'll be here then. If you're home . . . well that would be nice. I'll say hello."

He smiled to let me know things would be all right. Then he took the "warning" out of my hands, tore it in half, and trotted back across my yard to his truck.

I went into my kitchen and realized that since I now had to come to terms with my expanding world of job opportunities and men—Apollo, Jamie, Peter, and Lawn Man—it was time to go through my snail mail, which had been piling up for weeks. And where was my welcome from Starbucks?

Wait, what is this registered letter from Lending Tree? I have no account with Lending Tree. I scanned the letter and began to feel panic. They were confirming my request for a 250K line of home equity credit, and they were making sure the 75K "instant" cash portion was being sent to the right address.

I called the customer service number provided and was on hold for ten excruciating minutes. In that time, I got an email from Harper attaching the registration tickets to the Mobile Media Marketing tradeshow he wanted me to attend at Lincoln Center next week, a text from Peter asking what time he should pick me up tonight, a text from Hannah asking what I had decided about Jamie, and a text from Jamie asking essentially the same thing.

The customer service rep picked up. I told her I had no interest in a loan, had never asked for one, and had never applied. She read back to me my social security number and my mother's maiden name. How the hell did they get that? Even my mother would be hard pressed to come up with her maiden name.

She said the loan had been applied for online. I couldn't believe this could be processed without a signature. She said when the income is as high as mine (was), there is enough equity in the house, and the request is below 300K, it can be done online as long as they have the PIN, the maiden name, and the social.

My identity had been stolen.

She was savvy and super sweet and she walked me through the procedure of killing this loan request, but she made it clear I had better move quickly. Things began to hover, darken, and close in around me. I'm not even sure if what I said next I actually said out loud.

"You want my identity? Take it. Maybe you can make it work."

Okay, whom could I call to deal with this financial crisis? If I called my dad I would risk the stent from his angioplasty caving in, if I called Peter it would take me twenty minutes to explain that Lending Tree was not a yoga pose. I wasn't about to call Harper. I tried my own CPA but got his machine. I had no choice: I had to call my sister Jill.

"I don't get it," she said. "Hold on, we're at swim practice. I told you to bring your goggles. What would you like me to do now if you left them home?"

"Look, if it's a bad time—"

"So you borrowed how much? 250K! Honey, did I not say you could not continue to spend as if you were working?"

"Okay, Jill, try to focus. I didn't borrow any amount. My identity has—"

"This comes at a really bad time. We have two mortgages on our place; we have the note on all the new equipment Todd needed to stay current. I'm not saying we don't want to help—"

"Jill! Save the 'doctors are not made of money' rant! My identity has been stolen."

I walked her through the chain of events. Finally she locked in.

"Okay, here's what you do the minute we hang up:

"Close all your accounts. You don't know what's been tampered with, so close everything. Call the bank and see if they attempted any charges or withdrawals. Your guys seemed like online pros trying to pull off bank fraud, so you're probably okay; they wouldn't have wanted you tipped off.

"Contact one of the three major credit bureaus (Equifax, Experian, or TransUnion; they talk to each other) and place a fraud alert. Then they won't be able to do it again.

"Request a copy of your credit report and review it and look for suspicious charges. You aren't responsible if you find them and report it.

"File a police report right away. They won't catch them, but you'll have less issues if you need to prove it happened."

"Wow. Okay. Thanks. You rock. How do you know all that? Was your identity stolen?"

"Oh God, no, I would never let that happen." She laughed.

"Okay, Jill, I didn't *let* it happen; it happened. It's not a sign of my universal ineptness or your superiority."

"I'm just saying when you're a mom, you are more aware of things."

"How do you do that? It's amazing. You make everything bad that happens to me about me not having a child."

"You know," Jill said, impersonating my mom dead-on, "you are Sheila's godmother and favorite aunt, and she had a birthday party last week, and even though you are not working and not traveling, you didn't show."

"What? Really?! I thought her birthday was next week."

"I didn't think you'd remember that. I lied. That *was* a total Mom move. Whoa. I'm sorry."

"It's okay. When I find out who has my identity, I'll see if they'll throw in yours for the hell of it."

After I went through Jill's list, I decided to be happy that I dodged this bullet and to become a better human being *instantaneously*. As proof of my new solicitude, I remembered to close the finicky garage door with the remote attached to the wall. All Starbucks needed was that one-foot opening and she'd be off on an adventure. My vet says there is no reason a cat ever has to go outside, but nobody ever seems to explain that to the cats.

I then remembered that I still hadn't paid Starbucks any attention amidst all the chaos I came home to, and I started my way up to the study where I knew she was sleeping on the nubby blanket I lay out for her on the corner futon.

My phone was vibrating before I could even get out of the kitchen. I checked the number. Peter.

"Hi, I'm sorry for not calling you back about tonight. I came home to some issues."

"I left three messages."

"I know that. I believe I just said I was sorry."

"I was at work, but I still found the time to call you. You can't find the time to call me back?"

"What is it you think I do all day, Peter?"

"No idea."

Peter, trust me; you don't want to do this. You are out of your depth. "Well, let's take today. Today I got a call from a bank telling me someone had stolen my identity and was trying to get 250K in my name, thereby ruining my credit, and so I have had to deal with that."

I decided to leave out the tiny matter of Jamie and the not-so-tiny matter of Apollo. "250K! Holy crap!"

"Just to give you some sense of scale, Peter: 250K is the equivalent of you training clients all day every day and then multiplying that times forever."

"Look," he said slowly, "I know you have a big interview coming up and you are stressed—"

"Forget it. Look, let's take a pass on tonight."

"No, I'm coming over and we're going out. I'll be there at seven."

"No. I'm not up for it. I'm not trying to punish you, Peter. I just want to be alone."

"That's not fair, Casey. We had plans. I'm picking you up at seven."

"Not unless you want to keep your streak of consecutive restraining orders going."

"Wow. Okay, well, you win," Peter said softly. "I don't want to come over anymore."

I stood on the deck and tried to gather myself. Donald and I chose this house mostly because it backed up to a natural preserve of five hundred acres. We thought it was so great that no one could ever build behind us. Now I am making my isolation worse.

Regret was gnawing at me. Do I go out with Jamie now that I have freed up my evening, or is that a silly knee jerk to Peter?

I sent Harper a text that said simply, "I'm sorry to bother you, but I need another chapter. Now."

Harper called back just as I opened the door to the study and found that Starbucks was not asleep on her favorite blanket. This meant she was in one of her other hiding places. I asked Harper to hold for a second and called out to her in a falsetto voice that alternated her name with a fast, repeating smooching sound. Harper sighed, and it was rude, but I didn't feel like chasing her.

"Give me my chapter, Harper. Dating and interviewing. They are exhausting. How much is too much? Why shouldn't I play out the situation with Wallace and with Peter? And if they don't work out, then I'll start over. If that's wrong, I need to know why."

"Okay," he said. He still sounded tired.

HARPER'S RULE
Covering Jobs

All good headhunters 'cover' jobs. This means simply that every time headhunters accept a search assignment from a client, they send the client a short list of three to five excellent candidates in as fast a time frame as is possible given the parameters and complexity of the search. Studies show that if you 'cover' a job within a couple of weeks, the chances of a completed search are almost 100 percent.

Why?

1. There is a rhythm to hiring. If the clients interview every other day for a few weeks, the candidates stay centered in their minds, and the momentum continues. If too much time elapses, they can't remember the candidates as well.

2. Closeness of comparison. When you interview a candidate in close proximity to his competition, you do a better job of comparing strengths and weaknesses.

3. If you liked the first candidate, interviewing four others quickly makes you feel you didn't react emotionally to the first person you liked.

4. If you liked the first candidate, seeing others quickly allows you to have a choice without the fear of losing the first candidate.

5. If the hire is urgent because the work needs to be done, seeing a short list of strong candidates quickly comforts you that you didn't hire someone who is not right for the company long term just because you needed the work done.

While Harper was talking, I began to search for the hiding Starbucks. She was not in the bathtub in the master bathroom. She had to be on my pile of sweaters in the hall armoire.

"Are you saying, Harper, that if I date more than one person that I will do a better job of comparing? That proximity brings clarity? That I will feel that I made a more informed choice?"

"Yes, but it's deeper than that. You'll perform better too—date or interview. And do you know why? Because you will care less! Here is one of my cardinal rules of interviewing:

Candidates who interview like they don't need a job will almost always get the offer before candidates who interview like they do need a job.

"You want to get Wallace's job? A couple of interviews with other companies will only make you sharper, more comfortable with the flow. And you know what? That may come in handy, come offer time."

"Because I'll obviously have more leverage if I have two offers?"

"Sure, but not just that. You're missing the single most important reason why you should have multiple interviews and multiple dates:

The thing that can make a headhunter either deliriously happy or suicidal when a candidate calls back after an interview; the reason why the business is never dull; the most important rule of all: you never know.

"It's that simple. The interview you went on for the hell of it turns out to be an amazing opportunity. The company that seemed too far to drive to or that had too small a market share turns out to have a CEO you find awe-inspiring and visionary. Everyone you meet at the interview makes you feel like you've worked there for years, and even though it was never your intention, even though it was a throwaway, even though it didn't seem like a fit—"

"I end up taking a job that didn't seem right for me because I gave myself a choice."

"Exactly, and let's not forget one other thing: you have to look out for yourself. You don't have a job offer yet, and to my knowledge, no one has asked you for a commitment in a relationship. It could all disappear tomorrow. Choices protect you."

I could hear Hannah asking me how I knew for sure Peter wasn't seeing anyone else. According to Harper, he should be. "It feels cold, Harper, like I'd be misleading, whether it's a guy or a company. Someone gets hurt just so I can have a choice?"

"Choice is the core of free will. It's only when you truly have choices that you make the best decisions for yourself. And Casey, what is best for you is by definition best for whomever you'd be working for or trying to love. A sense of obligation fades, kiddo.

You can't be with someone just because you wish you were the kind of person who could be with someone."

Was Harper talking about Peter or his own marriage? It applied to Peter, though. He was good and kind and wanted a family and would never hurt me. I wanted to want Peter. "So you're saying I should go on the interviews and date others?"

"I'm saying I cover jobs, and I never regret a thing."

"What if I end up taking another job besides InterAnnex? Won't you regret that?"

I made my way down to the basement, to the antique nine-foot pool table with leather mesh pockets in the center of the room. We bought it near the end of our marriage. No one has ever played pool on it, and now the emerald felt is covered in Maine Coon fur. I turned on the light, but she wasn't there.

I felt myself starting to panic. I had a sense that Harper felt he was saying something critical to our discussion, but I wasn't listening. I started throwing cushions around and opening drawers she couldn't possibly be in.

"No, I won't regret it if you take a job through some other means. Here's what you need to know about regret: we are *fantastic* at forgiving ourselves when we act and it turns out to have been the wrong call; we feel regret when we decide not to act at all. I acted—I sent you to a client. If it doesn't work out, I will forgive myself much more easily than I would if I chose to wait before sending you out and then found you took another job. Casey? Are you there?"

I was back in the living room looking under the sofa where I had already looked. I headed back to my bedroom to make sure Starbucks wasn't under the blankets or in the hamper. I tried to stay calm, and keeping Harper talking somehow felt like it would help.

"I'm listening, Harper. Didn't want to interrupt you while you were preaching."

I hadn't let her out. That I knew. I would never. Then I saw that I had closed the door to my walk-in closet, one of her favorite places. Mystery solved. My shoulders dropped and I could breathe. The poor thing has been in there for hours; she is going to be furious with me. But why didn't she cry out? She couldn't have been sleeping this whole time. I opened the door to free her—she wasn't there.

"So the bottom line, kiddo, is when I cover jobs and candidates cover themselves and give themselves choices, they are protecting themselves from what we call in my office the Sixth-Month Stretch."

She was gone! Oh my God, where is my baby? I felt my hands getting clammy and a buzzing in my ears.

"Harper, I . . . I don't . . ."

HARPER'S RULE
The Six-Month Stretch

In every job and every relationship, the initial six months is fundamentally false: you are on your best behavior. So much to learn about an office culture, its tempo, its system flow ... nothing is redundant or boring. In the first six months of dating every story is being told for the first time, every place you go is the first time you have been there together, every move you make sexually is unknown and yields dividends.

It takes six months for you to realize those three moves were his only three moves. At work you now realize the job is kind of boring and reminds you of all the people you grew tired of at the job you left. When the Sixth Month Stretch comes, and it comes for us all in work and love, you will find it much easier to accept *if* you know you didn't settle. *If you acted and made a true choice, you will never feel regret.*

The garage door! It wouldn't open more than a foot. I meant to close it right away but then Lawn Man, the ID scare ... oh God, that was *hours* ago. She has never been out more than a few minutes; she could be miles away. I screamed, flat-out, primal. I threw the phone down without even hanging up and ran outside, calling her name as I went.

You don't feel regret for things you did, Harper? Only for things you didn't do? Well, I just let my cat out. My world. A creature that is completely innocent and who loves me unconditionally has now been let down by me, as has every sentient being before her who has tried to love me. I did that, Harper, and you know what? I regret it already. So you go to hell. Oh, God, please let her be all right!

I had already rescued her once; I had to keep telling myself that.

Donald and I had walked through the aisles of cages at the Humane Society to make our choice. I noticed a cage tag that read, maine coon!!—the only tag with exclamation points. This one was what they called a "Russian Blue": deep grey, with white streaks under her chin and on all of her paws, as if she were wearing gloves to offset her outfit. One of the volunteers, no doubt trained to pounce when there was interest, told me how sad it was that nobody wanted a purebred Maine Coon just because she had a "funny eye." And now that she mentioned it, the cat's right eye was funny: watery and lighter than her other eye. The volunteer shrugged and said people just don't take damaged pets. We left, thirty minutes later, with the soon-to-be-named Starbucks in tow.

We began our life together with a rescue, I kept thinking, now so far from the house I could barely see it. It would only be right if it happened again. But the light was fading; it was getting chilly. Damn it, Starbucks, where are you?

Every salesperson knows the mantra: keep yourself in the mind of the customer. I tried to imagine what Starbucks would be thinking as she ventured into the woods for the first time. I had no idea and was wandering aimlessly. I yelled out to her over and over and tried to keep the panic out of my voice. The thing that scared me most were the coyotes. I yelled at Donald about them so much he would interrupt me, "I *know*, honey, you don't have to say it every time I open a damn door." But I was relentless. And why not? Nine cats in three years in our neighborhood killed by coyotes. We all told ourselves lies: "They come back days, sometimes weeks later. You hear those stories about pets making their way back home from cross country." Yeah, right.

It was nearly dark. I decided to go home, get a flashlight, and call everyone I knew to come and form a search party. Oh, God, if I lose her . . . I will have to kill myself. Is that unprecedented? Would I be judged insane? I'm just so tired of loss. I've been trying to tell myself I have only lost things that I didn't care enough about to save, things that I didn't really want, but it still hurts. So how can I be expected to survive if I lose the one thing left I do care about, the one creature I have no ambivalence about? There would be no bouncing back.

I heard a rustling in leaves about two hundred feet to my left. I saw something disappear behind the cluster of birch trees. Was she just playing because she knew once I brought her back in she wouldn't get this chance again? Doesn't she realize the torture I am enduring?

And then I heard them. Coyotes don't bark or growl. It's a long, meandering moan. Patient. Like an echo. I started to feel sick.

She was so stupid to trust me. Didn't she know? Hasn't she been paying attention? This is what I do. I am not to be counted on. I cannot sustain things like love or work. I let go. It's just that I don't always let the ones counting on me know I've let go. You screwed up, little girl; you should have stayed at the Humane Society and took your chances on someone else taking you by week's end. For the first time in my life, I wanted to die. Not for drama or attention, but for the cessation of despair. I felt myself surrender. I stopped calling her name and made my way toward the house as best I could.

I didn't feel shock when I came out of the woods and saw them on the deck steps. I distinctly remember the first feeling I had was how comfortable a scene it was, how right it seemed. He was stroking her back as she lay stretched out in his lap. I could hear her purr of bliss ten feet away. He smiled at me and looked up at the stars.

"Nice night," he said.

"Harper, can I please have my cat?"

He handed her over, which did not make her happy, and I nearly smothered her. I buried my face in her fur and cried, and Harper was gracious enough to look away and say nothing.

"How?"

"You mean how did I find her? You freaked and went running in the woods, right? But if they've never been out, they don't go far. She was in your neighbor's garden."

"I meant how did you know?" I asked, my voice normalizing.

"Well, right as I was working up to my chapter's denouement, you screamed her name and didn't come back on the line. Also, in an early draft of your résumé, under career objective you wrote, 'to never let my cat out.' It was pretty obvious."

"I'm going to feed her. She must be starving."

"I already did—the IAMS can on the counter."

We sat quietly for a few minutes. I rocked Starbucks. The night descended. A flicker of a family.

"Know what the worst part was? The thought that shamed me the most?"

"You thought about getting another cat. It had just happened, and yet there was a part of you that was already finding a way past it."

I nodded and then the tears came back, but this time in convulsions.

Even when we met for drinks to celebrate the two times Harper had placed me, we had never embraced. Now he put his arm around me and squeezed. He kissed the top of my head lightly, as you would a child, and whispered that it was all over; it was all okay.

"Sorry," I said. "I must seem like such an idiot to you. On so many levels. Such a drama queen."

"Can I ask you something, Casey, something I probably should have asked a long time ago?"

I decided not to trust my voice and what it might give away. I nodded as gently as I could. I wanted him to know it was safe. That I felt it too.

Headlights briefly enveloped us in a stage tableau.

"That would be Peter," I informed Harper.

Peter bounded out of his car, puffed his chest up, and starting pointing at Harper. I couldn't even find the energy to get concerned. I suppose if nothing else I should have worried about Harper's welfare, but I could tell he was equally unconcerned. He was, if anything, bemused.

"We had a date!"

"Which I broke, and I told you specifically not to come over."

"Well, I decided to come over anyway!"

"You have to remember," Harper offered, tapping me on the shoulder, "he's not good at showing restraint, unless you draw it up legally."

Peter's face fell.

"You told him? You told him the most personal thing that has ever happened to me?"

"Actually, I told her," Harper said. "Headhunter. It's kind of what I do."

"Peter, you've heard me talk about Harper Scott."

Peter leaned over the steps, bent down, and got in Harper's face. Harper looked up and smiled. There wasn't a hint of fear.

"Peter, the rooster act can, in certain circumstances, be very effective. Even attractive. But given what I'm doing here, this is not one of those times."

"What are you doing here?" Peter demanded.

"Starbucks got out," I said. "I was on the phone with Harper when I realized it. Harper came over and found her for me."

Peter ran his hands through his hair, a sign of frustration I once noticed at the gym when he had to tell a client for the tenth time how to do a triceps kickback.

"On the phone with him. We had a date, I called you three times, and you couldn't call me back, but his call you can take?"

Harper whistled out loud. "Seriously? You don't get this yet? You are only going to make it worse until you accept that this day, the whole day, is about the cat."

Peter looked at me. I shrugged, then nodded. Harper nodded. If Starbucks were awake, I'm sure she would have nodded.

Nobody said anything for what felt like forever. Then Peter got up and started for his car. He opened the door, then closed it and made a beeline back to me. He got down in a baseball catcher's crouch. His eyes were glassy.

"It's just that I want to be the guy who finds her for you. That's what I want."

"Now see," Harper said, pointing his keyless remote at his Porsche, a chirping followed by lights flashing and doors unlocking from one hundred feet away, "that wasn't so hard."

I handed Starbucks to Peter and told him to take her inside. I caught up with Harper just as he got to his car.

"Harper, you've been good to me, but today was next-level. I don't know what I would've done."

"You would have found her. I just facilitated."

"You never asked me the question you said you should have asked a long time ago."

He looked behind me in the general direction of the house and just shook his head. He got in his car and drove off.

Back inside, Peter was mixing newspaper with kindling in the fireplace. He kept his back to me as I sat on the couch.

"So that was Harper, huh? He's in good shape . . . for his age."

I laughed.

"You mad at me for coming over when you told me not to?"

"Yep."

"You need to know I'm going to lobby really hard to stay tonight."

"I know."

I smiled, lay back, and stared at the antique white mosaic ceiling tiles Donald and I had paid far too much for, and felt something unemployed and lonely people seldom get to feel: I felt safe.

A Trade Show (in Theory): A place a group of vendors congregate during an industry conference to brand themselves and sell to a target audience.

A Trade Show (in Reality): A place where candidates find jobs under the cover of education and networking.

Harper burst my bubble of safety Monday morning. He told me we were focused on getting the InterAnnex offer, but we could take nothing for granted. I still had to go to the Mobile Media Show at Lincoln Center, and I still had the TradeHarbor interview on Wednesday, the day before I was scheduled to meet with Wallace and his board members. I asked Harper why I needed to go to a trade show when I had two interviews—one a final— already scheduled.

"You need the practice. You've been out of the game. You need to dial into the energy, reacquaint yourself with the technology. Half of the companies from last year's show are out of business. You don't even have a damn iPhone. Don't tell me you know what's going on. Besides," Harper added, a sly lilt in his voice, "it will be a good test for you."

"And exactly what are we testing?"

"You'll see. And did you happen to notice who was in Booth #173 at the show, and if so, why haven't you complimented me on my nuanced plotting and economy of energy?"

Harper had sent me the layout of the exhibition hall, but I hadn't looked at it yet. It turned out TradeHarbor, the very company I was set to meet with, was exhibiting.

"And I happen to know that Mark Porter, the guy you are going to be interviewing with, will be at the booth. You get it?"

Sure I do. I introduce myself after visiting the booths near his, let him take a look at me engaging with the competition, gathering intel, looking fabulous and dialed-in, and with a little luck and showmanship, he gets the message that I have other job options, thereby increasing my leverage. Nicely played, Harper.

"Will InterAnnex be there?"

"No, they are keeping everything on lockdown until the buyout. But listen, trade shows are invaluable."

"So, why aren't you going?" I asked.

"Oh, I wouldn't be caught dead at one of those things. I'm not wandering around all day having pointless conversations."

The thing I miss most about the phones I grew up with is that there is nothing satisfying about hanging up on someone now. They just think they lost the signal. But I did it anyway.

As I drove down the West Side Highway, I had to confess I was excited to be back in business clothes and going to a tradeshow. Here are the rules: First, you drive in. Trade shows last all day; you want to be able to leave when you want. Second, comfortable shoes. Whoever said there is no such thing as dress flats never worked a trade show. Third, tons of extra business cards. You will run out after giving them to losers and then the one contact that has promise will write you off as unprofessional because you can't give him/her a card.

Maybe the practice *will* help my interviews because I'm oddly nervous, even though I am one of 3,500 attendees and technically don't have to actually do anything but schmooze. But I could feel I was getting closer to being back in the game. I missed it. As I got near the entrance, I removed my show pass and hung my badge around my neck as though it were an everyday necklace.

Within an hour of walking the aisles, I realized Harper, had he deigned to grace us with his presence, could have had another chapter.

Trade shows are like clubs: If you are alone and don't know anyone, you stand there with a phony smile frozen on your face, trying to reassure everyone that you picked this particular spot on the open floor to stand. You are not alone or lost, you are calibrating when and if you want to give up this extraordinary piece of commercial carpet. You can only fake this for so long and then you have to 1) check your cell for messages, 2) go to the bar, or 3) talk to someone.

A former colleague of mine, Dean, in any social circumstance, would say, "How you doing?" knowing it would get asked in return; his reply was always, "Living the dream." It was flawless; it made everyone smile, whether they took it literally and thought he was fresh off the fire walk at a Tony Robbins seminar or realized he meant it ironically.

I got some coffee, chose the paper cup option so I could go mobile, and strode up to the TradeHarbor booth. I told Mark Porter I recognized him from his website and that I was looking forward to the conversation Harper Scott had arranged for us. Then, before he could react, I made a beeline for the next booth. For a full thirty seconds, I was the only registrant out on the actual exhibit floor. By the time I got to the end of the first row, I looked behind me and here came the sheep, their courage now bucked up by my intrepid journey. It gave me hope that what I originally thought, lying in my bed as a teenager, still might be true: I was different—special somehow. All the ensuing evidence to the contrary notwithstanding, this morning I felt that I might still be proven right. In any event, I got this party started.

Within an hour, I had my game back. I knew just by hearing a few paragraphs of their pitch if a company was underfunded—stay away from them. I also could tell by asking some direct questions who was here to position themselves to be sold. Consolidation was what it was all about for some of these companies: they didn't want to get big; they wanted to get bought so they could get big on someone else's dime.

An hour later I stopped at a kiosk to see the day's event schedule. Standing right beside me was a young man on his cell whom I'm sure was in his late twenties but probably got carded routinely. He had managed to read my name badge without me catching him staring at my chest. "How are you, Ms. Matthews?"

"Living the dream," I said.

"You know," he started, as he began to walk with me without asking if he could, "I have a friend who says these things are like the dating scene."

My God, I thought. Is your friend named Harper? "I'm Marty Rankin, by the way."

He held out his badge as if to prove he was giving me the correct name. It read "Silver Patron" on the lower right hand corner of the badge. That meant he was not an attendee, but either a paying sponsor of some portion of the show or some other sort of honored guest or dignitary. He motioned to a table and pulled out a chair for me. His phone buzzed and he turned away to take the call. I speed-dialed Harper.

"Quick. Marty Rankin. What do you know?"

"Uh, what do you want to know? He owns a company called CallShare. He invented a piece of hardware that attaches to your phone and enables you to record the call as an email file. Eliminates standard phone monitoring equipment. He's a wunderkind, like twenty-four or something. I think CallShare was last valued at 300 million and Google is rumored to want them to incorporate it into the Google Voice suite, which means they'll be worth three times that. Why?"

"I'm having coffee with him right now."

"Why would he be at that show? That's not his market space!"

"Don't know."

"Casey, he's Spielberg! He's Gates messing with Windows; he's Bezos not being able to find a parking spot at the bookstore! He's ducked my calls a hundred times, and I wish he was a client. If he has a job in your world, you forget about me and Wallace and you take it. You hear me?"

I hear you, Harper. Thank you, and damn you for not letting me keep my illusion that you don't really care.

Marty sat back down, apologized for the interruption, poured the entire contents of four packages of Sweet'N Low into his coffee, and smiled at me.

"I'm in a love coma," he said.

"Beg pardon?"

"I met a girl in Thousand Oaks where I live about eight months ago. Now I have a hard time focusing on business, let alone anyone else. Sorry."

"If you're in a love coma and you don't want to be harassed about business, why does a guy who owns a hardware-dependent company like CallShare show up at a mobile media show?"

"I'm the keynote speaker tomorrow."

"Oh, well, that's cool."

"No," he shook his head like a Labrador come ashore, "I'm scared to death. Twelve hundred attendees, and I've never done a group bigger than our office staff before. So I figure if I make some friends and buy some coffee, I'll have at least a few people who won't boo or heckle."

"You picked the wrong girl. If you sucked, I would boo and heckle. I don't applaud for coffee."

"How about breakfast?"

"For pancakes I'm a seal. I clap and spin a ball on my nose."

The pressure and the whole façade faded quickly once Marty told me flat-out he had a great sales team, and that he was trying to find his next CFO. He didn't have a job for me, which meant we could actually talk. No sexual pull making things complicated. A wonder boy is still a boy. He was utterly gangly, the geek not yet indoctrinated into the real world of adults, but among them all the same. So instead, with the games over, we had a real conversation.

I asked him how a love coma felt. I told him my situation. I said I was in the early stages of dating a great guy, but that I hadn't had any other serious relationships after my marriage. I said I had an interview coming up with a great CEO, but I still felt unsettled. I wanted to be in love, too. What was it like?

Before he could answer, my phone went off, but it was Peter, and part of our new post-coital covenant was that I would take his calls. We made small talk, and I was reminded that it doesn't take long being alone to miss the comfort of being a couple.

And then he blew it.

"So," he said casually, as if he were asking me about the weekend weather, "I'm thinking after you get your job this week, you need to break it off with Harper Scott."

"What did you just say to me?"

"Don't get sore," Peter said timidly. "Why would you need him once you have the job, right?"

"Where is this coming from? What has randomly brought this on?"

"It's not random. I just . . . look, I'm going to come clean because I want us to be able to talk about this stuff. I went through your phone during the night, I saw the amount of text messages and emails and how far back they went, and I just . . .'"

If Marty were not there, I think it's pretty fair to say I would have smashed the phone on the café floor. Instead, I neatly touched the red END CALL icon, gathered myself, and smiled at Marty.

"Early-Stage Dating Guy?" he asked.

"Right. Well, we clearly aren't in a coma, which is good because I would unplug him."

I was suddenly both furious and embarrassed that in the middle of the night, after we had strenuous-but-get-over-yourself-not-so-great-sex, Peter told me his version of the restraining order story. He was leaving, the fight was over, she threw his softball gear into the driveway, a ball rolled out of the bag toward him, he threw it against the brick edifice, it caught a corner and caromed sideways. Her face split, blood flowed, paramedics . . . restraining order. He was so, so sorry. And I believed every word when I should have been thinking, "He's got a bag of softballs with my name on them!"

"Let's change the subject, Marty."

A few minutes later we were saying goodbye. People walking by probably thought I was helping some intern. He would no doubt never know this kind of anonymity again, and I wondered how he would survive the next few years and the burden of absurdist wealth. When I tried to wish him well on his speech, he shrugged and asked about my interview. When I explained, his face widened.

"Wallace Avery? Oh that's too cool; he's an icon. I took a class from him."

Ooh! Information I might be able to use on my interview! My expression invited him to go on.

"It was a weekend gig in Cambridge, a symposium called 'Technology Startup Myths.' He blew us away. Two twelve-hour days and he had the most energy in the room."

I told Marty I would mention to Wallace that we spoke, and he said Wallace wouldn't remember him.

"There were like twelve of us. I never introduced myself or said a word. You can tell him this, though. He gave us a ton of corporate documents for free, and I remember our lawyers saying his non-compete was a thing of art. Airtight . . . You okay, Casey? Did I say something wrong?"

"No, no, you just reminded me of something I need to get done before the interview with Wallace. Multi-tasking, sorry. You're very cool. Good luck on the speech."

"You sure you can't fake being a CFO for me?"

I let him get about five paces, called out his name, and reached in my purse. I handed over the one business card I had.

"Harper Scott," he said, looking at it. "I think he's called me."

"He's the best, Marty. Really."

"You're the worst, Harper Scott."

"I'm sure I told you there was a non-compete."

"You didn't, because I would have told you that I wouldn't sign one."

"Why not?"

"Because they're inherently unfair. What if things don't work out?"

"Then you'll be unemployed. Oh wait, that's what you are now!"

"Harper, go to Wallace and tell him I need him to waive the non-compete or I'm not interviewing."

"No. Casey, listen to me. That will kill this deal. You're putting a gun to Wallace's head."

"Everyone knows non-competes don't hold up."

"That's not true. Mark Porter tell you that when you mugged him this morning?"

That was Harper's way of telling me he knew I had acted out. After leaving Marty, I marched over to the TradeHarbor booth and told Mark I was being courted by Inter-Annex. Did he want to do our interview right here and now? He said he was game, and we spent the next hour telling each other lies. Porter was a pure sales guy; all instinct and street smarts. He would never have the acumen of a Wallace. But he had no non-compete. Or was that a lie too?

"I would think you'd be pleased," I countered to Harper. "You sent me here to make things happen, and I have. He wants me to meet the CEO next week."

"You can get that job, but you don't want it. You want the InterAnnex job. You decided to make Wallace jealous by getting attention from TradeHarbor. You're better than that, Casey."

"Don't turn this into a tidy metaphor for your book. I am unemployed. I was told by someone *other* than my trusted headhunter that I will have to sign a non-compete, so I reacted by aggressively pursuing an alternative."

"Casey, there are perfectly good reasons why companies have non-compete agreements."

"Harper, I was married. I had the ultimate non-compete. You can't make someone stay when they want to leave. And you shouldn't be able to. You tell Wallace I said so."

"No. I want you to think about it. I want you to go home and chill and let me talk you through this before we kill this deal and you regret it."

"I gave Marty Rankin your name for a CFO search. You should call him."

"I know. He already called me. We're meeting. Thank you."

Of course Marty called Harper already. The most accomplished Type As are the quiet ones; while you are talking about what you're going to do, they're nearly done.

"I should have told you, Casey. I'm sorry."

I don't know if I would have even noticed the sign if I wasn't mad at Harper about the eleventh-hour non-compete issue now standing between me and the InterAnnex job. I was on my way toward the elevator bank when I saw it. The sign was a reminder of the lunchtime raffle benefiting MACY, the Mayor's Advisory Committee on Youth. The sign instructed us to visit the MACY booth near the atrium.

I couldn't imagine Harper's wife would be at the booth, but if they paid enough for the show, it probably meant someone from MACY got to introduce a portion of the program, and this might be something Maggie would be asked to do. I headed toward the atrium to get a look. But wait—what am I going to say if she is there? "I am a candidate your husband has placed several times and has known for years." Then again he has been to my house and, as Peter would attest, we are in contact nearly every day. I am also the chief muse of his ongoing attempt to write a book.

Maybe I would say all of this to Maggie and she would laugh, apologize, and then tell me that there were a dozen women like me in Harper's life at any given time.

I located a MACY volunteer and asked about Maggie.

"She isn't with MACY anymore."

"What do you mean?"

"Is there something I can help you with, Miss . . ."

I had taken my badge off and put it in my purse.

"I thought she ran the whole thing? She's all over your Web page."

"Is she still? Well, our IT budget is kind of limited."

I told her I was a friend of the family and that I had heard there was some *incident.*

"You must not be a very close friend of the family. She has been on a leave of absence for a month. Whom should I tell her showed so much *genuine* concern?"

No dear, we won't play it that way. Now you'll have to tell Maggie that the girl who was asking about her was younger, and you'll have to concede polished and even attractive, and while you'll reassure her I was not as skinny as you're sure I'd like to be, we both know she'll stop listening after the word *younger.* "Never mind," I said brightly.

Is this what Harper wanted to talk about the night he rescued Starbucks? If Peter hadn't pulled up, would we have spent the whole night talking? Would we have had the courage to cross the line and not go back? Would we then always regret spoiling that rare thing: a friendship between a man and a woman where no holds were barred, nothing was held back, nothing stored and bargained with later? Truth without consequence?

The entire walk to the parking garage I was in a daze. Has Maggie left Harper? And why? And even if she had, why would she have to quit MACY? And where was Jesse living? And how long has this been going on? Wallace said Harper had "a rough time of it." That implies months—years maybe. I felt angry. Here I was trusting Harper with my livelihood, with intimate knowledge of my relationship with Peter, and he trusted me with nothing. He took—he didn't give.

"Casey Matthews, right?!"

She was sitting on the bench in front of the attendant's booth, waiting for her car to be brought around. She still had on her badge from the show, but her name was covered by her coat lapel.

I got a moment's reprieve to remember who she was because the parking attendant asked for my ticket. She seemed to be about my age, but I couldn't tell. Her posture, her energy, her world-weary voice said older, but her skin was flawless and she had high, firm cheekbones. Who is her surgeon? I'm booking him now for when my time comes.

"I'm DiDi Cooper. We've met a few times, had lots of phone conversations."

"Oh, right," I said, recovering poorly. "Sorry, it's been a while. I recognized your voice but after seeing everyone at the show, I'm on networking overload."

She burst out laughing. It wasn't a nasty laugh. She was amused at how haplessly I was handling this situation.

This *couldn't* be DiDi Cooper. She was, and I assume still is, Harper's biggest competitor, and she positioned herself as a crass contrast: in your face; not educated but street smart. Her stock-in-trade was the outrageous remark, the inappropriate reference. She was the girl at the wedding who was smoking cigars outside with the boys. But in a lot of circles, especially at the C and V level, she was considered too lowbrow, too old school to trust with the upper echelon searches. Harper admired her tenacity and loathed her style. "Don't get me wrong," Harper would say to his clients, "she was great back in the day. A legend."

"Now why are you here, sweetie?" she said. "Rumor has it you are going to InterAnnex."

"It's not my first rodeo, DiDi. Until I have an offer in hand, I keep my options open, and that includes coming here."

"Of course," she said, impervious to implied insult, "goes without saying. Let me ask you this, if I had another opportunity that might be as appealing as InterAnnex, would you interview through me?"

God bless her. Relentless. If a neutron bomb was detonated in Manhattan right now, out of the wreckage would come DiDi, disheveled but not beaten, looking for survivors who might have business for her.

"I don't think so."

"Still one of Harper's girls. I get it. I love that man. Lost deals to him a million times, and my heart still breaks for him with all he's dealing with."

This was my chance. DiDi not only knew the whole story about Harper's personal life, but she would be only too glad to share it with me. But in the instant before I began to ask her to unravel the mystery, I remembered what Harper had said to me about going to the trade show.

"It will be a good test for you . . . you'll see."

He knew we would have to deal with the non-compete issue and that my problem with non-competes was visceral. Trust can't be achieved by signing a document, whether it is a marriage license or an employment agreement. It has to be real, it has to be earned, and it has to survive tests.

Donald's breach had done a lot of damage; I saw that now. The test was at the heart of Harper's book—as true of jobs as it was of relationships.

Harper's Rule: We have to continue to trust after being hurt by those we trusted.

When Harper wants me to know, he will tell me. If that's never, then I will have to accept that.

"DiDi, I really don't feel comfortable talking about Harper's personal life, or mine, or yours, for that matter. Take care."

"All right, honey. Listen, if things don't work out, I mean with Wallace, you tell our boy Harper you're going to give DiDi a shot. He's not afraid of a little competition, is he?"

In small doses, I could love DiDi Cooper. She is an unapologetic survivor. The longer I have been alone, the more I admire that. I don't know if she still has that gnawing, cold fear in the middle of the night that I have, telling me that I will be alone forever, that everything is passing me by, but if she does she has learned how to quell it and go back to sleep.

Several hours later, I was on the couch, wrapped in a blanket, sipping tea, and trying to convince myself to read the Alice Munro novel I had been nursing for over a month. I decided to check my Blackberry yet again before bed, and for a second I couldn't find my phone. I was about to tear the couch cushions off when I remembered I had stuck it in the back pocket of my jeans. I saw that while I was sitting on the phone, I had inadvertently dialed Jamie Post three times. Was this God's way of saying grow up and call the man back? But what was I going to say? That he was dodging a bullet by not getting involved with me? That yes, there was a spark, and I did feel some sort of connection on the train, but it wasn't real? It's real I don't do, at least not so much. Before I could decide how to handle Jamie, a red light signaling a new email flashed on my phone. Thank you, Harper. Distract me. I will call Jamie later. I promise.

HARPER'S RULE
Dealing with Non-Competes

There is a mythology about non-competes that I have to dispel for you. Like any myth, stories are passed on from one person to another, for years and generations, and everyone assumes it has now become truth, even though there is a conspicuous absence of evidence.

Let's start with the Big One, the one I hear all the time: "I can sign a non-compete because everyone knows they don't hold up."

Untrue. Believe me, as a headhunter who has lost countless deals because an ideal candidate has signed a non-compete, I wish it were true. But when you do the due diligence of researching the case law, here is what you find:

- Much of the time the company wins some relief or judgment.
- If you willingly signed the non-compete, you will be sued personally, and your new company will be sued as well (often resulting in them firing you rather than risking a lawsuit).
- You and your company will incur legal costs to defend yourselves. Depending on the case, this could range from 10–75k.
- It will take time and energy to defend, will cause resentment from your new employer, and will increase performance expectations.
- If you lose completely, you can't work for the new company, and you have to fight the old one. You'd better have money put away.
- Reference-wise you will be branded as someone who breaches contracts. Word gets around. You haven't just burned a bridge—you blew your bridge up.

But wait a minute! I remember a dozen times when someone went to work for a competitor after leaving a company known to have non-compete agreements. Ah, sorry Harper, should have kept reading . . .

The myth remains because sometimes a company chooses not to pursue because they don't think the candidate is a threat. Sometimes a small company doesn't have the resources or the legal budget to go to war. And sometimes they "plea bargain" and cut a deal.

But most of the time, when a non-compete is not pursued, it is far more human. We can all tell horrific stories of what happens when someone finds out a spouse has "broken the non-compete" and found another. But once in a while the pain is far greater. So they opt for dignity and grace. They say "go" and they ask for nothing. Their friends call them fools, but what they are really saying is, "If you don't want me anymore, then I will let go, because that's what someone who loves someone does." Clients with ironclad non-competes sometimes choose not to enforce them because they have broken hearts.

Was Harper speaking only from his experience as a headhunter? Or was this analogy about Maggie? Had she broken their non-compete? I told myself to snap out of it. I had a business judgment to make with Wallace Avery.

Enforceable? Yes, if the company follows the following tenets:
1. The *duration* is limited. Courts prefer six months, but for senior-level positions a year isn't uncommon.
2. The *scope* of the agreement is limited. Courts don't mind if you say someone can't work within fifty miles or work for a direct competitor, but if you say they can't work within 500 miles for any type of manufacturing concern, the courts will not enforce.
3. The relief sought is *definitive*. If your agreement says you owe 10K if you solicit customers you found while under the company's employ, courts will likely agree; if the relief is vague or exorbitant, courts will not enforce.
4. You have access to *trade secrets* that could damage a company's revenue stream or affect market share.
5. They don't seek *injunctive* relief. An injunction means you can't work for the new company until the non-compete issue is resolved. Contemporary courts are biased toward the "right to work." They don't like making anyone stay home.

Okay, Harper, I know companies have to protect themselves, and I have always understood that as a salesperson what I was being taught was essentially "intellectual property." But how do I keep them from exploiting me, using what they call "golden handcuffs?"

Non-competes are generally *not* enforceable:
1. If you are fired. Courts don't like to let companies have their cake and eat it too. If you let me go, I have to make a living and can usually go where I want.
2. If you signed the non-compete under duress. Non-competes are signed before you start working. If they make you sign a year or two later, it is implied that you will be let go if you don't sign, and that is duress.

3. If there is a material change in your compensation, job function, or ownership of the company.
4. If you are forced or asked to do anything illegal or unethical.
5. If your employment tenure was short. No one will hold up a non-compete when you were there six weeks.

As much as I found the idea of a non-compete distasteful, even un-American, I had to look at this in a more businesslike way. Non-competes aren't chains. I guess what bothered me was that I had Wallace on a pedestal, and this disappointed me. Why, if he was going to be such a phenomenal boss, would he need non-competes?

HARPER'S RULE
Motivations of Companies to Enforce

When I ask most general counsels or CEOs, they tell me non-competes send a message to those who remain. They need to know they will be sued and that management takes the non-compete seriously. But I find, like all business decisions, it is deeply personal. If you, as many do, leave an electronic trail after you leave that makes it clear you have been 1) interviewing for months, 2) talking about this to colleagues on staff, 3) dissing the company you are still collecting money from, 4) lying straight-faced about having some personal problem when you were in fact interviewing, and 5) looked your boss in the face when he asked why you seemed unfocused or distant and told him he was imagining things, and then give notice and go to a competitor, you have not just breached a non-compete; you have played someone for a fool. This is no longer about the reasonableness of restrictive covenant law; it's about misleading people who care about you. So they take the only action they can, a business action, and they tell their lawyer to commence a lawsuit.

Do I encourage my candidates to sign non-competes if they are part of my client company's standard process? Yes.

When I can't sleep, I need bad TV. The first channel I turned on was the local news, and the weather forecaster, an overexcited guy with an ill-fitting blue blazer and no tie (When did the local news go biz casual?) was exhorting us to go outside and check out "the rare blue moon in the sky tonight." It turns out a blue moon is not blue at all but just a really bright full moon. But I didn't move. There is, of course, no logical reason why a single person living alone can't go out and look at nature's gift of a blue moon. It's not a couple's thing. But I didn't leave the bed.

I called Harper. I looked over at the digital readout on the clock and it was after eleven. I expected to get his voice mail.

He sounded wide awake, the same Harper I get at the office.

"I called to say I read your chapter on non-competes. But I didn't have to. I pretty much knew after the trade show I would go along with it."

"Understood."

"Sorry to bother you so late."

"Not at all. I never miss a blue moon. They come once every 295 days."

"No wonder it's blue. I'm in bed."

"Well, get out of bed. Go to your window. Now would be good. Are you watching it?"

"Hmmm . . . okay, conceded. It's pretty awesome."

"Yes, it is."

"I like that we're both watching it at the same time. That we are seeing exactly the same thing."

"You and I always see the same thing; that's how we roll."

CHAPTER ELEVEN

ENDGAME— FINAL INTERVIEW PREP TO START DATE

Tomorrow I have my final interview with InterAnnex. If all goes well, I could be employed by week's end. Whether it goes well or not, I will turn thirty-five by week's end. People are weird about birthdays. I remember Hannah freaking when we turned twenty-five; the idea of a quarter-century on the planet made her feel ancient. For me, up till now, I was aware of the significance of certain age milestones only because I was being teased or questioned; it didn't resonate. But today was different.

When the well-wishers started calling to wish me luck tomorrow—my dad, Hannah, Jill—I found my mind wandering. I asked Jill to hand the phone to my niece Sheila, knowing her worldview would not include suggesting I get some rest and "give them hell tomorrow."

"Let me ask you something everyone's asking me lately: how old are you now?"

"Almost seven."

"Ever wake up and think, geez, I'm practically to double digits, what have I done? What is it all for?"

"Sure."

And I cracked up. I just don't have it in me to dwell on my age. Time to focus on tomorrow. The one thing I'm sure of is thirty-five and working will feel better than thirty-five and unemployed. Time to begin my pre–final interview ritual—to get in the zone. No one can define it, but everyone knows what it is: time slows; you are unaware of distractions and able to focus completely. When you are in the zone, you can't lose.

Every top-notch salesperson has been in the zone. Your well-rehearsed script comes out as if you just thought of it. You handle every objection with poise, and you seamlessly integrate your energy, your product's benefits, and the needs of the client into a tight, cogent presentation. You feel charged with energy. You have no idea how much time you have been talking. You just know you are "on." And they love you.

There is such a thing as an interview zone, and it can be summoned! But you need to create a ritual so that the zone finds you. I have never failed to get an offer when I summon the zone!

Ritual #1: Assemble my look

I always wear the same outfit. Every woman executive knows there are certain rules: no pants suits, nothing too flamboyant (go with navy, black, or grey), closed-toe shoes with no more than two-and-a-half-inch heels, a silk or cotton blouse, and go easy on the make-up and jewelry. So, while some day early in my tenure at InterAnnex I might walk in with my Tahari deep lavender skirt and my hot pink and black blouse, tomorrow I need to summon the zone. So I carefully removed the dry cleaning plastic from my Armani Collezioni navy-with-white-pinstripe suit with the three-button jacket, notched collar, and pencil skirt. I laid it on my bed and chose a simple ivory silk blouse. This was too conservative a look for my favorite black Prada shoes, so I went with my Giuseppe Zanottis, mostly because they had never been worn. Part of the ritual is to lay the entire outfit out on the bed, visualize the power the look will imbue in me, and then rewrap it and do it all over again in the morning. I never try it on.

Ritual #2: Watch my movie

To summon the zone I have to watch *Dumb and Dumber*. The first time was an accident. I couldn't sleep the night before my first big final interview, the zone was nowhere in sight, and I wandered through cable and settled on this 1994 Jim Carrey comedy. Is it a great movie? Of course not, but I no longer need the whole movie, just the one scene that convinced me I could get a sales rep's job that I was obscenely underqualified for nine months out of college. Jim Carrey confronts Lauren Holly with the burning question:. "What do you think the chances are of a guy like you and a girl like me ending up together?" She tells him they are not good. He asks for a percentage— one in a hundred? She looks him in the eye and says, "More like one out of a million."

"So you're telling me there's a chance!"

I search on YouTube, and the scene is there in its entirety. I have decided I am not violating my ritual if I watch the scene online and not on my DVD player. Even karma has to get with the times.

Ritual #3: Listen to my music

For me it's Barber's *Adagio for Strings*. My first interview ever was in Manhattan, and I drove a deathtrap of a LeBaron with 170,000 miles and moody brakes, so my mother insisted I drive her car instead. On the way in, I heard her CD with Barber's astonishing and thrilling piece. By its soaring end, I felt stronger and smarter: the music made me feel the interview was no longer the most important part of my day.

I got the CD out and put it on the kitchen counter near where I hang my car keys. I never listen to the piece unless I am en route to a final interview. I once ran out of an art gallery like it was a bomb scare because Barber's *Adagio* began to play.

Ritual #4: Go see Selma

Selma is a psychic. Laugh if you want; I was once cynical too.

I found Selma the day before an offer interview. I decided to kill time by going to a Bikram Yoga class. When I got to the little strip mall, I saw the sign for the yoga studio and a smaller sign that simply said PSYCHIC, NORMAL ROOM TEMPERATURE. I loved that. I found myself knocking on the door. A woman answered, and she looked absolutely luminous. Selma had on a black turtleneck and jeans; she looked like Carole King on the cover of my dad's favorite album, *Tapestry*. When I asked if she took walk-ins, she said, "There is no such thing."

And for ninety minutes she freaked me out. She knew things she couldn't possibly know. Within a few minutes she said she knew I had something big going on the next day, but I was not to worry, it would work out.

Selma puts me in the zone.

Ritual #5: Do my final check-in/prep call with Harper

In a world where you can find jobs posted on the Web and through social media sites like LinkedIn, it is not until you have had a few jobs that you realize even if you don't always need a headhunter at the front end, they are critical to securing the job on the back end. The final prep is different than the initial, generic prep. Now we drill down: who else is interviewing me? What are their biases or frames of reference? What concerns will I have to address? Harper tells me what they will ask and what I'm up against, and I get to rehearse, even role-play with Harper if I'm unsure what my response will be. You only have one shot at this job. No do-overs!

I got on the Merritt Parkway and headed toward Selma's, and en route I got two calls from Peter and one from Harper. I just didn't have the energy for Peter, and Harper could wait until later; you cannot mess with the order of the ritual. First Selma, then dinner, then a bath, then Harper's final prep! Don't these people read my memos?

I didn't overreact when I saw that the strip mall had been expanded and updated. The Yoga Center was now One-Stop Yoga Mart. I tried to stay calm and told myself that Selma would have some great stories about the renovation, but when I opened the door to go upstairs to her office, there was no upstairs. The receptionist said the "earthy crunchy" lady had left when the building was sold to the owner of the yoga studio.

How could Selma do this to me? My basic sensibility about business was affronted.

If you are going to make a move, you let the clients know! I could feel the zone choosing the "unable to attend" response to my InterAnnex RSVP. I was a fool to let myself begin to hope. The hope is what gets you.

I drove home, I ran a tub of hot water, I added my favorite bath salts, and I used the Bat Signal: I texted Harper. He called me almost immediately.

I gave Harper the lowdown on my ritual, my zone prep, and Selma's disappearance. I told him I realized this must all sound silly to him.

"Absolutely not," he said, "except for the psychic. That *is* crap. She may be a lovely person, Casey, but she is a fraud."

"Hmmm, funny . . . When I told her about you, she called you my vocational guardian angel."

"I take it back; she's special. We have to find her."

"I can't go on the interview, Harper. It's all going to go wrong."

"We cannot cancel. Half the senior management team is flying in just to meet you."

"Harper, I believe in my ritual. I believe in the zone."

"Okay, well, time to drink a different Kool-Aid."

"You don't get it! You control your world. But it feels like nothing works for me the way it used to."

"Casey, you have to go on the interview."

"I know."

"Good, then suck it up, and let's prep. Do you have a Quest Diagnostics you can get to first thing in the morning? You need to do a blood draw and urine test."

This was not part of the usual final prep. I told Harper there was one near my gym, but I had never been there.

"Go there tomorrow. They open at seven. Don't eat anything after midnight."

"InterAnnex is doing a drug test?"

"Yes, but not just you. There is another candidate, a guy the venture capitalist knows, and they are testing both of you."

"Do you know anything about him?"

"Why do you hurt me? I know everything about him. Go to Quest and give them the InterAnnex address and sign over permission to send the results to Wallace."

"Okay."

"Casey, for the record, do you have anything you want to tell me where a drug test is concerned? Now's the time."

I suppose he had to ask. I wouldn't be the first unemployed person to take comfort in recreational drugs.

"Not unless they test for red wine." I wanted to know since when companies drug tested before an offer was made, but he was already beginning to launch into his checklist for the final prep. I knew this stuff by heart, but especially with Selma's apparent abduction by aliens, it wasn't time for another alteration in my ritual. I soaked in the water and listened to Harper's voice, telling me what I already knew and still needed to hear.

HARPER'S RULES FOR FINAL PREP, #1

Know who the players are. You will likely be meeting with people you have not seen on previous interviews. Google them, of course, but also go to the company website and read their bios, see if they are on LinkedIn or Facebook, or if they have a following on Twitter. Remember that they often have an agenda different than the person you will be working for or even the person running the company.

Dead on, Harper, I thought. In my case the problem is the money guy, John Sabia, their primary venture capitalist. Harper said he was an unusual guy, which was code for "he's not Wallace and probably won't like you." Sabia made a ton of money in gaming technology and later reality television, and has made 800 million dollars from his last three startups. He is pushing for the other candidate.

"All I'm going to tell you," Harper said, "is push back when you need to. He's got a big ego and is used to getting his way. I haven't met him, but I hear his midlife crisis is of epic proportions."

"Got it. I am going to assume Wallace hates this guy?"

"Yup. But not enough to not take his money, and nowhere near enough to tell him he wouldn't consider the other candidate over you."

HARPER'S RULES FOR FINAL PREP, #2

Corporate Carpe Diem: Go over your accomplishments and achievements and be prepared to document how there is a direct link between 1) where you have expertise and 2) their short-term problems.

Companies will go on poetically about their desire to build toward the future and hire talent that will complete this lofty vision, but in the end, in the overwhelming majority of employment situations, companies hire short-term solutions to short-term problems. They are focused on *Now*.

I'd already compiled a list of major accounts I opened with brand-new products. Startups burn cash and need revenue; it's no doubt the biggest reason InterAnnex wants me.

HARPER'S RULES FOR FINAL PREP, #3

Role-play concerns about your candidacy.

This is not the time to rationalize or make excuses or hope they don't come up; they will. Open the closet, look at the skeletons inside that make up your life, and be prepared to answer the obvious negatives. Remember, this is a final prep. They already like you, and they are already predisposed to believing whatever you tell them as long as it sounds and feels authentic.

"You," Harper said cautiously, "have two areas I see as possible exposure: 1) you left a job without a job, and 2) you have never managed a sales force. How do you plan on responding?"

I told Harper I planned on blaming him for leaving my job since his avaricious and wanton ways created the reduction in my sales force that left me exposed and cast aside.

"Tell me," Harper sighed, "when will you be over that? Is there a timeframe? Can we set a date?"

I reassured Harper that I would play it straight. I was asked to stay on my previous job by the CEO, and a counteroffer had been forthcoming. I could still be there, but I felt it was a matter of integrity not to be taking their money while I was interviewing.

"Nice. And item two?"

My response would be that in a startup there really is nothing to manage, that sales VP would be a title only for a year or two, and that I presumed if they wanted someone who was used to sitting in an office and directing in a hands-off, strategic way, that I wouldn't be sitting there. I also told Harper that I wanted to subtly point out that they needed new blood.

Harper suggested an improvement:

"You should hire me precisely because I am *not* a manager. I am a clean slate. I have no bad habits, no preconceived notions. I won't irritate you by always saying that whatever you want me to do is not what I did back in the day. I have been managed and know how it works, and you, Wallace, are a great manager, an icon. One of the reasons I want this job is to learn how to manage."

"Okay," I said, "I love that. I remember now why I made you part of my ritual."

HARPER'S RULE
Ending Interview with the Big Ask

Ask for the job at the end of the interview.

Don't leave this to chance. Companies want to know where you stand. And if they are torn between two candidates, one of the deciding factors is often who wants the job more. Their reasoning is simple: the one who wants the job more will work harder.

When a company offers a candidate a job, it is the corporate equivalent to telling someone you love them. There is only one appropriate response. Anything other than responding that you love them as well, which in this case means you want the job, creates doubt. Leaving the interview without declaring yourself is no different than responding to the person who just said I love you with 'thanks, I appreciate that.' They know what that means: you either don't love them, or more likely, you love someone else.

Here's exactly what to say when you ask for the job: 'I want to thank you for your time today, and before I leave I want to make it very clear that I want this position. I would like to ask if any of you have any concerns about my candidacy that I can answer before you make your decision.'

If they say 'no,' then you say: 'Then I just want to discuss timelines. I have another option that is going to press me for an answer.'

If they say 'yes,' you should field the concern, try to overcome it, and then ask, 'Does that satisfy your concern?' If they answer 'yes' to this, then say: 'Can I count on your support?'

No need to discuss numbers or start date *unless* they do. If they do, they have played their hand, and the job is yours. Ask to see the offer in writing, tell them you will start as soon as possible, and leave the meeting on your terms.

"Got it, Harper. When does the other candidate go in?"
"He was in today. I scheduled you last on purpose."

Harper's Rule: The candidate who interviews last usually gets the job.

"Hey, Harper, is this going to happen? Am I getting this job?"

But Harper is not Selma and wouldn't play. I knew what he would say: "You make things happen. Or you let them happen to you."

Even though my commute would be twenty minutes longer, I was thrilled that Inter-Annex had their headquarters on Grand Street in Soho. I have always worked in Midtown, but I loved the Village and loved Wallace for still being cool enough to be there.

One of the signs of a quality company is when you have an interview and the receptionist has been prepped to receive you as a visiting dignitary. It shows they value talent. When I got to the front desk, the receptionist greeted me by name, asked if I wanted anything to drink, and generally made me welcome. I wasn't surprised, but I was gratified. As I expected, the first twenty minutes were spent with their human resources director. Thanks to Harper, I knew better than to take this lightly. "They don't have the power to hire you, but they have the power to derail your chances," he always said. The HR director ran me through the usual litany, verifying my work history, dates, and W2s. He mentioned they did a background check, and I took the opportunity to point out I had been to Quest this morning as directed. He could tell from my voice I was surprised that a drug test was being done before the fact. "We don't normally do it that way either, but Wallace said Mr. Scott insisted it was his firm's protocol." He shrugged as if to say it was too trivial for him to make a fuss over, but now I knew that Harper drove the preemptive drug test.

With HR in my camp, I was brought in to meet the board. It was a room that seemed designed more for defending a PhD thesis than as a conference room, but I suppose in essence that was what I was doing—defending my work. There was a podium and a side table set up opposite a long mahogany table, and Wallace and three gentlemen sat in overstuffed leather chairs. One chair was vacant.

Wallace explained to me that we were waiting—"not surprisingly," he said with an edge—for John Sabia. He offered me coffee, but I was already on sensory high alert, and when I add that to caffeine, I always have to pee. Not knowing how long I'd be stuck in there, I told him no, thanks.

A moment later, the door flew open and John Sabia practically jogged in. Sabia fist-bumped the CMO, CFO, and IT director, but Wallace stared him off. I judged him to be in his early 50s. His head was shaved, he had diamond-studded earrings in both ears, and he had a soul patch— heavily dyed black—under his chin. The tail of some sort of serpentine tattoo finished just above his clavicle. He wore a black Twisted Sister t-shirt, black jeans, and sneakers. His sinewy arms belied his potbelly. He was trying oh so hard to be hot. It wasn't working. Clearly, Sabia's midlife crisis offered a testament to the power of his money to prevent people from laughing at him to his face.

Malcolm Gladwell says we make decisions about others in a blink. Neither Sabia nor I even needed a blink. I kept hearing Harper's voice: "He's the money guy. You won't work for him, you'll hardly ever see him, and once you get his endorsement, you can spend all your leisure hours hating him. He is only relevant for the interview." The good news was that Wallace clearly loathed Sabia.

Wallace handed out a summary of notes he had made during my last interview, and he graciously added some of his own thoughts to my "unique strategy" and gave me full attribution. On paper, my musings seemed to be the fully fleshed-out work of a thought leader in the space, not the riffing of a relatively inexperienced executive.

Sabia balked. He said the guy they had in earlier worked in the social networking space currently and had done so his whole career. Why should they wait for me to come up to speed when he could hit the ground running?

I smiled brightly and said it was so refreshing to finally not be the "kid" in the interview process. Since social networking was nothing but dorm room dreams until 2003 and not a market factor until much later, if the other candidate had spent his whole career in social networking, he must be just out of school. And if he is qualified for this job, he must be "an amazing young tyke." Everyone laughed except Sabia.

The CMO, a cherub-faced guy named Harley with wiry salt-and-pepper hair, was eager for me to lay out my game plan. I enumerated what I considered the problems with the typical social networking business model and the inherent glass ceiling of "ad tolerance." Wallace broke in with studies and statistics to back me up that, of course, I had not researched. I concluded with my recommendations for marketing proprietary social-networking solutions tailored for the corporate clients who could most benefit from them.

Sabia pounced: Why hasn't this been done before? I didn't know. What would the first ninety days look like? I wasn't sure. How long before we would get our first sustained quarter of revenue? I shrugged.

"Meanwhile," he sighed with disgust, "I pour in money. A hope and a prayer."

The CFO, a guy named Vivek, reminded Sabia that just two months ago at their Montego Bay meeting, Sabia was bemoaning pouring his money into "just another social networking concern" and wanted a new marketing approach.

"I'm just saying my guy, highly recommended as you know, has got experience that, no offense, she doesn't have," Sabia countered. "He's *doing* it."

"He sits in London and directs a U.S. sales force," Vivek said. "He hasn't been in front of a customer in two years. How hands-on is that?"

Wallace interrupted to restore order. He was clearly embarrassed that they were talking about the family with a guest in the room. If this were *The Godfather*, he would have walked over and slapped "Santino" Sabia.

But Sabia didn't make his ridiculous fortune by caving in or by not getting his way. He conceded my idea had promise, but that didn't mean I would be the right steward. "Maybe we can hire you to work for the other candidate as sort of a VP-in-waiting," he suggested. After all, I had never managed a sales force.

"No, thanks." I said.

Wallace made it clear he saw no sales force beyond admin support in the first phase of the launch and that they needed someone who could sell now and manage later, not someone who used to sell but hasn't done so in years.

We were at an impasse. There was a full thirty seconds—an eternity in an interview—when we were all silent. I couldn't remember ever getting an offer when an interview came to a full stop like this. And then, wouldn't you know it, I was rescued. By Sabia.

"How old are you?" Sabia said.

I looked over at Wallace to see how to play this.

"You can't ask her that!" he said.

Sabia wanted to know why the hell not since it was his money that was providing, among other things, the conference room we were sitting in.

"Because it is against the law! How could you not know that?"

Sabia said this was the real world and he wasn't interested in legalese or games.

"Games?" Wallace said incredulously. "Let me tell you what you've just exposed us to. If we now hire your candidate, based on what you just asked, Ms. Matthews could sue us for age discrimination, depose all of us to prove what you said, and sue for all the money she would have made from us plus punitive emotional damages. A good lawyer would ask for somewhere around 50 million dollars as a starting point."

I couldn't help but think that suddenly the other candidate seemed like a great choice. But I decided to take the high road and secure my standing with Wallace and the others.

"Mr. Sabia," I began, "my résumé gives you the date I graduated college, and you can see I have had twelve years of work experience, so why would you ask a question you already know the answer to?"

He glared. "Straight up? Here it is. Without a strong sales force, this venture goes nowhere. This is mission-critical. You're of a certain age, and lady, I don't need you walking in here after you get the job and telling me you're pregnant and you quit."

Vivek covered his face with his hands. Harley apparently knew Wallace well, because he half rose out of his seat to see if he would have to restrain him. But Wallace didn't move; he just went cold—icy.

"That's enough. You've just broken another law," he said, his lips barely moving. "You and I are done. I can get funding without having to put up with your puerile nonsense. Casey, I'm sorry. This simply should not have happened."

It's not the first time pregnancy had come up during one of my job searches. I suppose I can take solace in the fact that, given my pending birthday, it might be the last. It was eight years ago, during my first big move with Harper after my rookie success. I had sailed through the interview process, was scheduled to go in for a "rubber stamp" meeting with my boss's boss, and while dressing to meet Donald's parents for dinner, I realized my breasts were sensitive to the touch of my bra, and they looked a little swollen to me. At dinner with Donald's parents, it suddenly hit me that I had not had my period in some time, though I couldn't say for sure how late it was. I barely got home without a full-out meltdown. If I was pregnant, was it going to cost me the job? Would they rescind the offer? Will they assume I will take maternity leave and not come back? Maybe I shouldn't tell them. Was that an awful thing to do? I sent Harper an email that said I was having an argument with a friend who might be pregnant, and I wanted him to settle it and tell us what legal responsibility she had to tell the company.

It took me half an hour to find the home pregnancy test under the sink amid the extra toilet paper and unused cleaning supplies. In the meantime, Harper called me back.

"Casey, were you asked on the interview if you were pregnant?"

"Could you at least have gone along with my pathetic story for a minute or two?"

"That is outrageous and against the law. I will call the CEO right now. The Pregnancy Act of 1978 is very clear. They can't ask you, and you don't have to tell. You can choose to tell them if you'd like, but you are under no obligation."

"No one asked me, Harper. That's not why I wanted to know."

"Oh . . . Got it."

"I'm not pregnant, as it turns out, which is an utter relief. I just didn't want to screw up my offer, and I sent you the email before I took the test and—"

"Casey, you okay?"

"Actually, why don't you go ahead and be sorry for me? Just in case?"

"You know," Harper attempted, "kids fully suck. Mine is on eBay as we speak."

"Save it, Harper . . ."

Wallace and the boys were waiting on me. Was I going to show outrage and leave to call my lawyer? Would I try to exploit the situation? What did Casey really want?— a question that has lingered for too long.

"Wallace, I appreciate your umbrage, which is called for, to be sure, but can I say a few words?"

They were in no position to be anything but a respectful audience.

"First of all, I don't want to sue for millions. I don't want to make money through lawyers because of some infantile behavior; I want to earn millions by doing what I do. So everyone can relax."

I moved over to Sabia and addressed him directly. I made eye contact and didn't relinquish it.

"Mr. Sabia, you and I will get along fine. You need someone who is not afraid to say something besides 'yes' to you, and you need someone who will occasionally call you on your nonsense, which I will do cheerfully. But that's not why I should be hired. You need me because I will obsess, I will drive revenue, and in so doing I will inspire a sales force and get you your investment back. You simply need to signify you understand that I am right by getting that smug look off your face and telling me you are sorry."

"Turns out I am," he said. "I was out of line."

"Forget it. You'll find I truly let things go. Know many women like that?"

A few minutes later Wallace escorted me to the lobby. He said he would never forget how I handled Sabia's ignorance and latent misogyny. He promised he would have an answer within a day or two, and he made it clear he wanted me to be his VP of sales.

"Sabia is going to fight you on this, isn't he?"

"The other guy did a similar venture for Jigsaw; he has some serious credentials. In a perfect world, Sabia would want you to work for the guy—as a way to get grounded."

"You mean a proving ground? Sorry, Wallace, I won't do that."

"So you said. Let me do my thing. Whatever happens, I think you're an extraordinary young woman."

"I appreciate that, Wallace, but that sounds very much like a consolation prize."

Wallace bit his lower lip and took a moment. I couldn't imagine what he was like at my age—insufferable, probably, in some sort of glorious way. Just my type.

"I'm seventy-one years old, Casey. I don't sell myself to anyone anymore, but for you, I'll say this: the next time I don't get what I want in a business deal will be the first time."

When Harper first placed me at Siebel Systems, along with the great training, the awesome branding, and the visionary management, I got to share a cubicle space with Drake. He looked a little like Gene Hackman, (think *French Connection*, not *Royal Tenenbaums*), and management was smart enough to realize his real value was passing on wisdom to aggressive young sales reps who saw the world in absolute terms. One day I asked him what was the biggest mistake he saw among rookies like me.

"You haven't committed yet to your career. Down deep you are waiting for a sign, for enough good things to happen to you to justify making a commitment. But it doesn't work that way. You have to commit first, and then, *because* you have committed, good things come to you."

I thought of him now. I decided to commit, in my mind and actions, to Wallace. He said he was going to get this done, and *because* I chose to believe him, good things would come.

The first proof of this epiphany would be the feedback I would get from Harper, and the sooner I heard from Harper the better my chances. I left him a text message saying I was anxious for his feedback and that I wanted to tell him about the craziness with Sabia.

I didn't hear back from Harper that evening and when I woke up, I reached over the alarm clock to my charging Blackberry and checked my messages. One was from Peter saying he hoped the interview went well and that at some point he would like to talk. I also had a Facebook invite from Jamie Post, who had now officially tried every form of communication. This one laid the guilt on thick. "Just do me a favor and let me know you're okay. I *get* that we're not going to date." I didn't want to call him back, but something was telling me not to let go.

By noon, I had left messages for Harper on his office voice mail, on email, and on his cell. At 1 P.M. I texted him to let him know that I assumed no news was bad news and that I was a big girl and could take it. At 2 P.M., starting to wonder if Donald's old scrip of Xanax might still be packed away somewhere, I went to the Jigsaw website, read the management profiles, and checked out my competition, a guy named Cameron. His education was better, he had been through startups, he had published several *New York Times* articles on the social networking phenomenon, and while it was never mentioned, let's face it, he was sporting a penis. That's unfair, I told myself. Wallace has hired many women executives.

The bell of my Blackberry rescued me from this self-absorbed rant. An email from Harper. "Casey: I got your multi-media barrage. You can stop now." This was a bad sign: bad news is easier to deliver in email. But I read on.

HARPER'S RULE
Waiting for the Offer
Waiting for an offer is the hardest part of the process. It makes candidates doubt their intentions. They begin to rethink. Their minds go to crazy places. This is very human and very *dangerous*!

The offer is the most important thing in your world. It is just *one* thing a corporation has to do. So you need to take a breath. There is no hidden meaning in the delay. I have made it perfectly clear to Wallace that every hour that goes by the more variables they are risking, like offers from other companies. I am exerting leverage. You have to trust me.

Right, trust again. The more people tell me I have to trust them the less I do. If someone were trustworthy, would they really have to tell me to trust them? Harper ended the email vaguely. "I won't be able to talk live, and I won't be able to check in via cell or text for a while. Not to be cryptic, but I have an issue I have to deal with. Wallace knows how to reach me when they have a decision, and I will check my email when I can. I'm on this. Try not to stress."

Now that I am officially thirty-five, I told myself, I needed to not overreact. It has been one day since my interview. It is a high-impact position with a startup company in a volatile market sector; there is nothing unusual going on here. And so what that Harper will be out of touch? He has a life beyond me, and I've known obliquely for some time there were issues he was dealing with, but I am sure he will still tend to

InterAnnex like the consummate pro he is. I am not going to freak. I decided this was all a test of my ability to commit first and ask questions later.

I made a decision. I am a good decision maker. I don't mean I make good decisions—I often don't—but I am good at making decisions.

I decided I could wait all day and die a slow death, or I could use the time to expand the notion of "commit first; good things come as a result" to all areas of my life.

I never even got into the gym to tell Peter that if I had two lives, I'd be happy to risk one on him; that I loved that he was kind; that I got it that he only wanted to take care of me and be happy and safe; and that I wanted to want that too. But that I didn't. At least, not with him.

Nope. So many times we stress over things, and we never even have to face them. Or if we do, they are never as hard as we imagined they would be. As it turned out, the parking lot was packed, I had to park in the last row, and as soon as I got out of the car I saw them. They weren't kissing; they weren't even standing that close to each other. But a woman knows. They laughed. They lingered. And they looked amazing together. She had something I lacked. She turned her head to the side and I could see it: she wasn't angry—about anything. I not only wasn't jealous, I felt bad about holding them back.

I owed it to Peter to wait for her to leave. He was such a good man. I knew there would be days, years from now, when I was angry at my spouse for dealing me some injustice, when I would wonder why I let such a kind soul go without a fight. And as I approached him I remembered what Harper told me when I left my first company. I had just landed a big deal; I had a huge commission check coming my way. If I quit now, I'd forfeit it. I wanted the new job, I told him, but should I really leave the money behind?

Harper's Rule: All candidates of quality leave behind something in the job that is good and worthy; otherwise, they'd never move forward.

Peter dutifully asked me about my interview, and I withheld. It no longer mattered. "Good, it was good. Thanks."

Peter took a breath, just like he does before he begins a set of shoulder presses. Gathering his strength. That is what I have been to this guy, resistance training. "So I know you're stressed about the job and the timing is not great, but like I said in my message, I think we should talk."

I slowly shook my head. "What I think works best is if I join another gym. Which means I probably won't join another gym, and then we don't feel awkward on a daily basis, and I get the bonus of blaming you when my butt gets squishy."

"I wish you liked me more, Casey."

"I like you plenty. That's not what this is about."

He was too sweaty to hug, but how do you not hug at a time like that? Besides, showering gave me something to do when I got home while waiting for Harper to call. Why do they call it "killing time?" Time was killing me.

When I checked in with Harper by email the next morning, I got an auto reply message for the first time in the near decade I've known him. It said he was unavailable, and if it was an emergency to call Leena. Now I was truly scared, but now for Harper more than me. For Harper, an auto reply message is like waving a white flag.

I grabbed my cell to call Leena but decided it was too early and called Jill instead. When I get stressed, I ask if I can play Rock Star Auntie and take Sheila off her hands for a few hours. Jill said there was a rock climbing party at the YMCA, and it would be great if I would take her.

Sheila thinks my sporty Audi is super cool. She played with the sound system joystick until a Pink song came on, and it was both hilarious and disturbing to hear her sing along with the lyrics: "I've never been this nasty . . ." She told me she loved the song, and a few minutes later she said she loved my car. And in the sudden demonic possession only a mother's influence can produce, I heard my mom say through my mouth that you aren't supposed to love things, only people.

At the "Y" I scored next-level cool points with Sheila by strapping on the rope and climbing the thirty-foot wall while the other adults watched with phony smiles on their faces. I had successfully gone nearly two hours without thinking about my job when I saw that Leena had tried to get me. I waited until snack time and found a corner spot where I could hear her.

"Mr. Scott got your message," she said in a rehearsed voice, "and he says he can't talk to you directly, but that we should know something today."

"Leena, you know my history with him. I'm worried about him."

I knew I was putting her in a tough position, but she was all I had.

"It's just bad timing," she sighed. "All I can tell you is the very big event in your life is coinciding with one in his life. He's doing the best he can. He's checked in with me and Mr. Avery twice today."

"Okay, then tell me this. Did they make an offer to Cameron? Is that what is really going on? They want Cameron first and I'm the backup?"

"Oh my God, that's not going to happen, I can promise you that."

"Why are you so sure?"

"Because we found out yesterday that you passed the drug test, but apparently Mr. Cameron did not."

Well, that explains why Harper insisted on the drug test. Once he found out Sabia had his own candidate, he went digging, discovered Cameron's potential "issue," and made the drug test protocol a part of his process, which forced them to have Cameron submit to a test as well. With the short notice he was unable to flush his system. Just in case Avery caved and agreed to hire Cameron, Harper made sure he had a failsafe way to stop it. I posed all of this to Leena.

"I don't think Harper—I mean, Mr. Scott—would want me to confirm or deny, but if I can speak off the record?"

"Please do."

"It's freaking brilliant, right? We all know you're the best candidate. Mr. Scott was just creating an insurance plan."

Sheila announced she would make me a deal. She would climb the wall faster than any boy, and I could feel free to count, as long as we got Dairy Queen on the way home. She seemed to understand that the ends justify the means; why was it so difficult for me to accept?

HARPER'S RULE
Receiving and Negotiating an Offer

An offer is two things: it is obviously an offer for work, but it is also a test of your enthusiasm. Remember, when a company makes an offer, it is the corporate equivalent of saying, "I love you." When you tell someone you love them, you don't want to hear, "Thanks a lot, I appreciate that, let me think about it for a few days, see it in writing and review my options, then I'll get back to you and hopefully say I love you, too."

I tell my clients to submit written or emailed offers for authorization, not consideration. By the time of an offer, they should be able to give an answer immediately: yes or no.

On the drive back to Jill's, InterAnnex human resources sent me an email. I tried to concentrate on Sheila. Time with her was precious, I kept telling myself. At the first stop sign, though, I decided that was crap, that Sheila was still a kid and at this rate might get a job before me. I asked her as sweetly as I could to give me a moment of quiet while I checked an important email. I opened it and saw that it was a formal offer from InterAnnex.

I went home and decided that I should print the offer. Somehow that made it seem more official. I didn't need Harper, even though he almost always negotiated the terms and conditions for me. It was my damn job and my damn life, right?

Dear Casey:

It is my great pleasure to formally invite you to join InterAnnex as the Vice President of Sales . . .

Wow. It happened. The Holy Grail. Vice President of Sales at thirty-five! (Okay, I cut it damn close, can I have my moment please?)

. . . your annualized base salary will be $250,000 USD. This will be reviewed annually . . .

Okay, that is SO much more than I expected! I want to call Hannah, and I am so excited I need to pee!

. . . you will be eligible for additional compensation . . . we will determine performance "gates," and once they have been exceeded, you will earn 2% of the total sale upon billing . . .

No waiting until the money comes in. Class move, Wallace.

. . . startups require ramp-up time, and in recognition of such, you will, upon execution of this contract, receive a sign-on bonus of $40,000 USD . . .

Shut up! Seriously, if I read this right, I sign this and FedEx it back and I get 40K tomorrow! Now I can't call Hannah and brag; the 40K is too much, she'll hate me, and I don't blame her. I'll just buy a new best friend.

I started to speed read.

Group insurance (includes life insurance, short- and long-term disability . . . you may contribute to a 401(k) and we will match 50 percent of the first 5 percent of pay . . . your main office will be in New York City, but as a VP you have flex time . . . you are eligible for twenty-five days of vacation in the first year and eight personal days . . .

And then the famous "airtight" Wallace Avery non-compete. I can't compete for eighteen months, can't solicit any of their clients, and can't recruit their employees. But other than the social networking space and its direct competitors, I am free. Fair enough.

This is so much fun! Why did I let Harper do this part? In fact, I think I want to be a headhunter and read unemployed people their offer letters all day. (Although I guess you also have to tell the runners-up they aren't getting a wonderful document like this. That would be awful. Okay, Harper can be the headhunter and I'll be the VP of sales.) Let's cut to the chase, sign this baby, and move on with my new life. I know Harper is a stickler about making sure it is an at-will agreement that either party can terminate at any time . . . Check, it's right there, in black and white. I suddenly felt none of my pens were worthy. I felt like I should have one of those pens presidents pull out when they are signing legislation they had to break arms and cut earmark deals to get through Congress.

And then, a surge of abject panic.

Where's the equity piece? Where's the part about me getting in on the act when they get bought out—the real money? I reread each page. Nothing about options, no language on grants, not even a purchase plan where I can devote some of my base pay to buy shares.

Nada. It's a rich comp plan for sure, but they can afford to be generous with the comp because I'm just a hired gun. They'll pay me 400–600K for the next two years, and then sell, and each board member will make millions. Whether the new company keeps me on board is a crap shoot.

What should I do? Should I email Wallace and politely ask him if the equity piece is coming in a separate attached document? Will that make him furious? Was I being ungrateful? My proposed salary of 400–600K is oh, about 400–600K more than I'm making right now. Should I sign it, do my job, and worry about it later? No, that is nonsense. It is standard for a VP of sales at a software startup to get an equity piece. I am being exploited.

Sorry Harper, I need you. I know you're involved with something heavy, but this is serious. The last line of my offer letter says I have to give an answer within twenty-four hours.

I left Harper a text and said I was in a Code Red—that Wallace had sent me an offer, but I have a deal breaker: no equity piece.

Harper's Rule: A deal breaker is a concern about a job, company, or boss so important to you that you would prefer to turn the job down rather than let it go unresolved.

So. Will I walk away if I don't get equity? Before I could decide, a text came in from Harper.

Harper's reply—"that's impossible"—reinforced what I knew at some level: that I was not creating drama. My phone buzzed.

"Harper, I know this is not a good time—"

"I'm going to call Wallace and get to the bottom of this, but you have to sit tight. I can't do it for another couple of hours; I just can't. Chill, okay?"

"Harper, I want to call him first. Not because I can't wait—or, well . . . not only because I can't wait, but if I'm going to be his go-to sales and marketing executive it has to start now. If I can't negotiate my own plan, why would he entrust me to negotiate with CEOs of large corporations?"

"Okay. You're right. Good luck."

I shut off my phone. I wasn't going to risk having this call dropped just as I was asking Wallace the hard questions. This was a landline call.

HARPER'S RULES

At offer time, keep in mind:

Companies will start low so they have room in case they need to increase your offer. They will also start by telling you there will be only one offer.

They will ask you, as an unproven contributor, to wait to receive certain benefits or compensation perks "once you have established yourself." But you must negotiate everything you want now. Once you sign, you're just another employee. The chase is over, the game won.

Let me just say this and be done with it: Wallace took me to school. He was polite, even affable, and he was happy to discuss it. But the answer was no. There would be no equity. I now wish I hadn't, but I had to ask him why he changed his mind.

"Because I don't think you deserve it, not coming in the door. Casey, this is a career-changing VP's job that we both know on paper you are not ready for. I believe in you, and I'm willing to take a risk. But the other board members asked me to limit that risk by having you wait for equity until you have become a proven commodity. I had to agree with them."

"Carrot and stick? Wallace, I didn't think you were that old-school."

"Well, then you weren't taking a very good look. Old school got me here. My advice is to take the job. But you think about it and call me tomorrow. The offer stands."

And he was gone. I grabbed my cell and went outside and sat on my front steps. A gorgeous day . . . if you're working. I phoned Harper.

I was proud that I rolled it out to him while remaining completely composed. I told him I didn't know what to do, that I wasn't sure he should call Wallace. It would just look like I went running to Harper for help, which of course is what I was doing, and it might weaken my position further. What did he think?

"I don't know," Harper said.

Huh? Since when? This was his sweet spot, this was my über-headhunter, and in my hour of need he doesn't know? What the hell is going on?

"Harper, you are scaring me. Are you all right?"

"No, kiddo, I guess I'm not."

I don't know who will do my eulogy when I die, but whoever does it will say that for all my flaws, I loved my friends ferociously. For so long, I've wanted to show Harper that side of me, and now I had my chance. "Harper, where are you? Right now?"

"I'm home."

"Let me come to you."

"No. I won't be here long. I have to be someplace."

"Then pick a place."

And he gathered himself.

"Okay, I should be done by six. Greenbriars in Greenwich is close to where I'll be. Meet me there, we'll put a strategy together, and then I'll call Wallace."

"Harper, the hell with Wallace! I just want to see you."

After we hung up, I took all I had not to drive to his house. It wouldn't be the first time. I remember the night, early in the Harper Era. A garden-variety tiff between Donald and me that was so minor the offending issue escapes me now. I stormed out of the house and went for a drive. I knew Harper lived on Lincolnshire in Greenwich. It was a cul-de-sac with only four ridiculously huge houses, and Harper's car, back then a silver Maserati coupe, was in the circular driveway. I was about to return home to face Donald when there was a tapping on my window that startled me so much I screamed. A hulking man with a high-pitched voice that didn't match his physicality one bit asked me if he could help me. Yes, I thought, you could stop stalking me while I'm trying to get some stalking done here. He lived next door. I had to get out of there—what if he asks my name or worse, if Harper comes out of the house—my life would be over. I made up a lame excuse about this being the only place I got three bars on my cell and I needed to call home. As I turned around in the cul-de-sac, a light went on in one of the front rooms. Harper had Jess, she must have been six or seven then, in his arms. She was sound asleep. He was taking her upstairs. I don't know what I came to see, but this was not it. I went home, apologized to Donald, and initiated make-up sex with an intensity of which I am not proud.

I have always had trust issues with other women, and that includes the woman who barks out driving instructions from my GPS system. She is way too serious for my taste in general, but if she tells me to take a turn the wrong way down a one-way street, and I value my life enough not to comply, she gets *shrill* and keeps repeating that I have missed my turn and that I must go back. I decided I couldn't take a chance on bringing her in on the Greenbriars mission, so I went to MapQuest on my laptop and printed the directions.

An hour later, if I turned the radio down, I could almost hear the GPS lady laughing. I-95 was gridlocked. My Blackberry, resting comfortably on my passenger seat, vibrated as if in response to the car horn's mating calls. Jamie Post's name flashed across the screen. Well, I can't keep ducking him, and I certainly have nothing else to do at the moment. Might as well take my medicine and get this over with.

"Jamie, let me just say it. I butt-dialed you. I'm sorry."

"Okay. I don't know what that even means."

"It means the phone was in my back pocket, I didn't realize it was on, I pressed up against something, it dialed your number. I'm so sorry."

"Why, of all the numbers in your phone, was mine the one it dialed? Wouldn't you have had to scroll to it and consider calling, or maybe started calling, and then chose not to, in order for it to even be in a position where it could be . . . .what did you call it?"

"Butt-dialed. Ask your daughter, I'm not making it up. And yes, I almost called you."

"To say what?"

"Jamie, I am stuck on I-95, trying to get to a meeting that could well determine a lot of very big things in my life."

"Okay, so let me help. I'm an engineer. I've been trained in how to determine big things."

There was something about how he said it. I found myself telling him to weigh in. "How does one determine big decisions?"

"It's simple. All the information about a larger entity can be found in a smaller piece of the same entity. You already know what you need to know."

"Meaning stop trying to make a decision by looking at the big picture?"

"Exactly. Take the smallest possible picture, and you can extract everything you need to know about the big picture from what it tells you."

I brought Jamie up to speed on my job offer. Was he saying that in the smallest possible element I could find my answer? That I already know what I need to know?

"Yes. Just like you know everything you need to know about me from a train ride and a butt dial. Bye, Casey."

I spent the next hour trying to distract myself by changing lanes and jockeying for position. I tried not to think about what Jamie said. But I found myself scrolling, highlighting, and after a deep breath, pushing my green SEND button.

"Hi, Wallace. I decided I don't need until tomorrow. I thought we'd both rest easier if we just resolved this. I'm going to turn down the position."

"I'm sorry to hear that. Because of the equity?"

I know Harper might be mad at me for doing this, but if what he says about relationships and jobs is true, then I'm doing the right thing. Wallace and I are in the infatuation stage. We'll never feel this way about each other again. If he can't commit to me now, how can I believe he will do it later when the daily grind exposes us both to be imposters of a sort?

"Thanks for everything, Wallace. You know you're going to miss me, right?"

"Have you told Harper your decision?"

"Nope, on the way to meet him."

"Two percent."

"What?"

"I will give you two percent of the company's stock coming in the door. Fully vested. Day one. Cisco makes their move, you hit a home run along with the rest of us."

"Really? Oh my God, Wallace, I don't know what to say."

"I would start with accepting, follow that up with a heartfelt thank you, and finish up by telling me I'll never regret it. But who am I to tell you what to do?"

"You're my new boss, that's who. Thank you, Wallace."

I managed to get off I-95 and into a mini-mart for directions. They involved going back part of the way I had just come. Had I not gotten lost, I would have met Harper at the restaurant. I am convinced life is so much more about timing than it is intention.

I had to do a technically illegal U-turn to circumvent the underpass and begin to backtrack. If a cop was going to nab me, he would be parked in the commuter lot just before the entrance, so I did a full scan before I proceeded.

And there was Harper. His Porsche was in the middle of the commuter lot, and he was standing next to it. There was a Lincoln Navigator parked parallel to his car, and behind it a massive U-Haul truck. Maggie was talking to the driver of the U-Haul truck. I knew I should leave and wait at the restaurant for Harper, but I couldn't. Not until I knew he was all right. I pulled over just before the lot entrance and positioned my car behind a pickup truck. I was out of their sight line, but they were in mine.

Maggie and Harper spoke for a moment. He looked down and then away, and then she moved in as if to hug him, but he stiffened and she pulled back. She motioned behind him, and Jesse got out of Harper's car. She reached into the jump seat and took out a backpack.

This was the dreaded drop-off: a ritual performed in commuter lots on Friday nights all over the country. This early in the divorce, a neutral place is selected to minimize advantage and lack of convenience. It is designed to make the parting less emotional.

A woman I used to work with dreaded Fridays. Her kids were little; the youngest would scream bloody murder and beg her not to leave. The start of the longed-for weekend for the rest of us was the beginning of her nightmare.

Jess put her backpack down and fell into Harper's arms, exhausted. They spoke for a moment, he said something that made her laugh, and she went to the Lincoln—a brave girl trying to ease her dad's pain. I would find out later that Maggie had found a new home, she had primary custody, and she was taking Jess with her. Harper would see her only on weekends from now until she went to college. They had spent the whole day at Harper's house loading up the remnants deemed necessary for Jess and Maggie to feel whole at their new place. A home they had built and shared for fourteen years was now looted in the purest sense, and Harper had to head home to it. And while this day had been coming for a long time—almost two years I would later find out—it was here now.

The truck and Navigator drove off. Harper stood by his car, folded his arms, waited patiently for the SUV and the U-Haul to get their green light and enter the freeway, and then, when he was sure they were out of sight, put his hands on top of his head and began to cry violently. I thought he was going to get sick, but these were just the arid convulsions of utter grief.

I had waited so long to see some side of him that wasn't protected, but I wasn't prepared for the other extreme. I opened the door to go to him, but another commuter, using the lot for more conventional reasons, rushed to him and was trying to comfort him. Harper waved him off. He needed something besides comfort.

I texted him. I told him that I had taken matters into my own hands since he was such a slacker. I told him that Wallace and I had come to terms and that I was the new VP of sales for InterAnnex, had full equity, and that I was grateful for all he had done. I hit SEND.

A few seconds later he took his phone out of his windbreaker, read my message, and broke into that crazy wide smile I do so love. He did a tiny fist pump in the air, and then rubbed his eyes, first with the closed fist and then with his sleeve. He looked twelve years old.

When he looked up, I was almost twenty feet away. I could tell he didn't want me to see him like this. He waved his phone and started to congratulate me, but then he surrendered. He opened his arms and burst back into tears as I wrapped my arms around him and waited out the shaking, the halted breathing.

"Please don't tell me it's going to be okay," Harper managed. "I've been saying that to people for twenty years. And it's not true. It's not going to be okay."

I nodded and said nothing, and squeezed tighter. Some things do not happen for a reason, are not for the best, and do not give you perspective. Some things just suck.

I got to Greenbriars first and asked for a booth in the back, just to save Harper any further embarrassment. But it wasn't necessary. He was composed. But, for the first time I saw the face of his father that was in that picture at the diner. Harper would age after all. Harper would die.

"Confidentiality is a headhunter's lifeblood, Casey. You know that, right? I've been holding back on you, and there are things you deserve to know, but I can only go so far. The details are between Maggie and me."

This grave and wholly unnecessary pronouncement was interrupted by a waitress and two waiters bringing over a cake with candles in it. They sang the tune of "Happy

Birthday," no doubt the extent of their play list, and substituted lame lyrics congratulating me on my new job. I glared at Harper. He shrugged.

"I thought we'd be celebrating because by now I would have made a brilliantly glib call to Wallace. Who knew you didn't need me?"

I blew out the candles, and the people near us clapped for me. I tipped my glass to them.

"Wallace was the lover," Harper mused. "He had no chance."

"What do you mean?" I asked.

"F. Scott Fitzgerald wrote that in every relationship there is a Lover and a Loved. One party loves the other more than the other party does. It's a dirty secret nobody admits to. Fitzgerald said you want to be the Loved, not the Lover. The Lover gets a broken heart, the Loved gets her heart's desire. You were the Loved."

And, it was clear to me, so was Maggie. The plot elements might change, the settings differ according to status, but it's all the same in the end. Harper began to sketch . . .

Apparently she met the man in Bloomberg's office; he was a promoter of tennis events, a nice guy, Harper conceded. Harper began to see the signs: the distancing, the brittle phone calls when Harper would call from the road, the slow cooling of ardor, the late nights out, with increasingly feeble justification. And that terrible period when you know but do not ask. You go to work, you concentrate on Jess. You tell yourself you'll write a book and help an old friend find a job.

Jamie was right—the smallest moment unveils the biggest picture. I loved Harper, but not in the way I thought. This crystal clear fact was astonishing to me. Then I did think of a question.

"So how did Wallace and DiDi Cooper and half of New York know you were going through a divorce? How did it go viral?"

"Oh. That. Well, early on, I was chasing rumors. I got some intel wrong and got it into my head that it was the mayor himself who was the paramour. I chose to address the matter while he was making a toast during a MACY meeting. It's kind of cloudy to me."

"That's fantastic. I would have given anything to be there."

"For the record, I would like to say I not only apologized but voted for the man."

Neither of us was hungry. We pushed our food around our plates.

"Why not tell me? Why the book?"

"I believe in the book; I've wanted to write it for a long time."

"But you were living it too. Why test it all out on me?"

"You're stronger than me, Casey."

"So now what?" Harper asked. "For the first time since we've known each other, we are both single. You now have a really good job, so I wouldn't be dating a loser."

I was going to start a rant about how much healing and grieving he still had to go through and how he needed time to be alone. But it felt completely flat and false. I just shook my head.

"Are you saying we're not going to even try? Casey, we're crazy about each other, you know that!"

And there it was. Right in front of me. I had landed my dream job and now my dream guy was mine for the taking. The perfect ending to Harper's book. And there was no way. The moments you wait the longest for are always a letdown.

"Harper, we're already exactly what we need to be for each other."

Harper braced himself. I could tell he was preparing his rebuttal. The waitress bought him time by dropping the check on the middle of the table. Harper waited until she left, smiled warmly at me, and for the first time in all the years we've known each other, he slid the check across to me.

Onboarding: The extended, proactive support process by which companies successfully transition executives into their new roles and organizations.

Wallace's onboarding process was professional and much appreciated. The way a company onboards you reinforces your feelings about your decision and fuels your desire to succeed.

He sent me a welcome package via FedEx, outlining how I could immediately enroll in the health and benefits plan. He sent out a press release to the *New York Times* and the *Wall Street Journal*, and he featured me on their website. He sent an IT guy to my house to deliver, load, and configure a company laptop. He set up lunch with my new executive assistant, a fiery redhead named Laney whom I love. He had a dinner in my honor at his home the Friday before I started.

Wallace was a class act. My job was well worth the risks of quitting my old job and being unemployed. Overcoming the fear of change has made me a stronger and better person.

In the first six months I exceeded my annual revenue goal. Cisco hasn't bought us yet, but if they don't, someone else will, and I will be one wealthy girl. And why not? Why not me?

The onboarding at home has also gone well. Thank God Harper finally started dating, because once he met Jamie they fell in love and began that guy thing of talking to each other and forgetting I was in the room. Politics, sports, nanotechnology . . . there was no stopping them. I knew I was completely over Harper when he got me aside one night when Jamie went to the bathroom and whispered, "You don't deserve him. Seriously, he could do better."

But now Harper and this hilarious girl Tia seem to be working out, and we are a team. Jess is the same age as Jamie's daughter Brea, and they text each other 500 times a day. I packed up Starbucks and moved in about a month ago. It was scary, but Jamie's cat of twelve years had died the year before, and he paid more attention to Starbucks than I did, and well, Jamie's house is awesome. There are no coyotes in the neighborhood.

Will we get married? I'm not even going there. Harper kids me about it all the time, of course, and I told him that he missed one of the ways in which jobs are like relationships. We get into ruts in both, but we forget that part of what we love *is* the rut: the routine, the sameness—knowing what you have. I'm going to enjoy my rut for as long as I can.

Harper published his book and dedicated it to his daughter Jess, and to me. He is back to full swagger again, and sometimes I miss the humble version. One morning Jamie and I were doing what people with a teenager do: playing chauffeur and heading to a lacrosse field. The commercial on the radio ended, and the host said, "And now we're here with Harper Scott, noted headhunter and the author of a new book called *Harper's Rules* that claims if you correctly learn how to find a job, you can also find true love."

Jamie got excited and told me and Brea to shut up—Harper was on the radio! We both rolled our eyes. Anything he was going to say, I told Jamie, I gave him. But the host asked Harper what he wished people would learn from his book, and I guess it's only fair to give him the last word, because it made me look at Jamie and smile.

HARPER'S FINAL RULE

If we used the language of work in our relationships, we'd have fewer problems and a lower divorce rate. We need to stop saying we "fell in love." Falling implies a misstep, a mistake. We would never say we fell into a job; we accept a job offer. We need to start saying, "I love you, I want to be with you, I accept your offer of love."

For now, and I hope forever, I accept Jamie's offer of love. And if it doesn't work out, well . . . I know a really good headhunter.

DATE DUE

Demco